Political
Theology

Political Theology

ELIZABETH PHILLIPS

t&t clark

Published by T&T Clark International
A Continuum Imprint
The Tower Building, 11 York Road, London SE1 7NX
80 Maiden Lane, Suite 704, New York, NY 10038

www.continuumbooks.com

British Library Cataloguing-in-Publication Data
A catalogue record for this book is available from the British Library

ISBN: HB: 978-0-567-18175-6
PB: 978-0-567-26354-4

Typeset by Newgen Imaging Systems Pvt Ltd, Chennai, India

CONTENTS

ACKNOWLEDGEMENTS

I would like to express my gratitude to the following people for the various ways in which they helped make the writing of this book possible: Westcott House and especially my principal, Martin Seeley, provided the research days and freedom during the summer months which gave me time to prepare and write. Jason Fout and Craig Hovey read and commented on early drafts of these chapters, and Samantha Stayte did the initial proofreading. My desire for this book to exist and my ideas for what it should look like arose largely from teaching political theology in the Cambridge Theological Federation, and I am grateful to all my students and especially to Anna Rowlands who has been my colleague in this endeavour for three years. My husband, Jeff Phillips, has been, as ever, my constant and supportive companion, encouragement, gentle critic and theological sounding board.

INTRODUCTION

My last vestige of 'hands off religion' respect disappeared in the smoke and choking dust of September 11ᵗʰ 2001, followed by the 'National Day of Prayer', when prelates and pastors did their tremulous Martin Luther King impersonation and urged people of mutually incompatible faiths to hold hands, united in homage to the very force that caused the problem in the first place. It is time for people of intellect, as opposed to people of faith, to stand up and say 'Enough!'[1]

—*Richard Dawkins*, A Devil's Chaplain:
Reflections on Hope, Lies, Science, and Love

[T]his historical moment of global transformation has provided an occasion for religion – with all its images and ideas – to be reasserted as a public force. Lurking in the background of much of religion's unrest and the occasion for its political revival, I believe, is the virtually global devaluation of secular authority and the need for alternative ideologies of public order. It may be one of the ironies of history, graphically displayed in incidents of terrorism, that the answers to the questions of why the contemporary world still needs religion and of why it has suffered such public acts of violence, are surprisingly the same.[2]

—*Mark Juergensmeyer*, Terror in the Mind of God:
The Global Rise of Religious Violence

It is not a claim which is new to our generation, but it is a claim which has been echoing with renewed vigour through the pages of scholarly and popular books, periodicals and websites since the terrorist attacks of September 11, 2001: the claim that when religion goes public, when theology gets mixed up with politics, things go terribly wrong. Look at Christian fundamentalists bombing abortion clinics in America, some will say. Look at the history of strife in Northern Ireland. Look at the interminable conflict in Israel/ Palestine. Look at George W. Bush and Tony Blair leading the West into war in the Middle East. Some people will pick up a book like this while browsing in their favourite shop, see the title and think, 'O God! The very *last* thing we need is more political theology!' For those who consider themselves to be without theological convictions or commitments, theology seems something very much better left to spheres of life other than the political. Keep it in your churches, in your private lives, in some classrooms (if you must), they say. And it is not only those committed to secularism or atheism who find the idea of political theology repugnant. For some who themselves profess theological convictions and commitments, the mixture of theology and politics is just as disturbing a thought. My faith is not of this world, they say. My faith is about spiritual, personal and religious things, not about politics.

And yet, theological claims and motivations crop up again and again in political discourse and in the political realities of our lives. Whether we are talking about going to war or the regulation of biological and genetic sciences or what governments should be doing in times of financial crisis, the theological is there. It is there in overt ways, such as the 'God bless America' and 'punish the evildoers' rhetoric in the United States or the Archbishop of Canterbury's public questioning of the government's budget cuts in the United Kingdom. It is also there in less overt ways wherever we are considering issues which involve the meaning and purpose of human life and human sociality, how we order our lives together.

Remember that 'the political' encompasses far more than the sorts of items which fall under the heading of 'politics' in the daily news. When Aristotle wrote *Politics*, it did not only cover questions like the best form of government or what rulers should and should not do; it was about what things make for the flourishing of human beings and how common life should be ordered in ways that promote that flourishing. Likewise theology is a wider category than what is taught in a Sunday school, a catechism or a course in systematics. It involves all sorts of questions about God, humans and their lives in relation to God, and all that which is ultimate. Thus, by 'political theology' we mean not simply those highly debated, current-event issues which might initially spring to mind like Islamic extremism or abortion. We mean something which is both more basic and more broad. In this book I will assume the definition used by William Cavanaugh and Peter Scott in their companion to political theology:

> Theology is broadly understood as discourse about God, and human persons as they relate to God. The political is broadly understood as the use of structural power to organize a society or community of people . . . Political theology is, then, the analysis and criticism of political arrangements (including cultural-psychological, social and economic aspects) from the perspective of differing interpretations of God's ways with the world.[3]

Thus, in one sense, political theology is entirely unavoidable. People's thought, discourse and practices related to political arrangements will inevitably be shaped by their thought, discourse and practices related to the ultimate and divine, and vice versa. It is also true that the political has been present in Christian theology from its very beginnings, and throughout most of Christian history church leaders and theologians have thought and taught about politics without seeing this as an entirely separate matter – of course theology would include political theology!

On the other hand, political theology does not come at all naturally. It is an aberration to atheists and secularists who believe that theology will always taint and distort politics. It is a perversion to those Christians who believe that their faith is only about that which is higher and less temporal than politics. And it is a discourse which many theologians in the mid-twentieth century decided had been ignored and neglected by generations of churches and academics alike, thus they issued the resounding call, 'Christian theology *is* political!', in the inception of the discipline of political theology.

Through this introduction I hope to remind students and scholars of theology and its various disciplines that before theology was carved up into the specialisms of the modern academy, the political was always understood to be one of the central concerns and topics of Christian theology; political theology is not a fringe interest of just one variety of theologian. I also hope to inform a wider readership about the connections between their faith, its history and traditions, and the political realities of their societies and lives. Our political opinions and practices will inevitably be shaped and guided by claims and convictions about truth, what is good and what is ultimate. If we are not intentional about making these connections, about allowing our politics to be guided by what is truly ultimate in Christianity, we find instead that our politics are conformed to ideologies which claim that someone or something other than the triune God is ultimate. The Christian church has always called such claims idolatry.

Though this book is an introduction to political theology as done by Christian theologians, it is important to note that the idea of political theology did not begin within Christian theology.[4] The Western ideas of the *polis* and the political originated in Athens and the philosophy of the Hellenistic city-state, where politics was seen as the science and art of seeking the common good. The Romans would build upon this tradition, and the phrase 'political theology' was first employed in the Stoic philosophy of ancient Rome, which distinguished between three types of gods and thus three types of theology: the personified forces of nature (natural theology), the gods of legend (mythical theology) and the officially worshipped gods of the *polis* (political theology). St Augustine considered and critiqued this distinction at length in *City of God*.[5] Indeed, one way in which Christian political theology began was through early theologians – and Augustine in particular – comparing and contrasting Christianity to the existing ancient traditions on political philosophy.

In the modern era, the phrase was brought back into use most famously (or infamously) by Carl Schmitt (1888–1985), a German legal and political theorist. Whether or not to include Schmitt in a book on Christian political theology, defined as work done by Christian theologians, is a contentious question. On the one hand, Schmitt insisted that he was not a theologian, and most of the scholarship done on his work has been in the vein of legal and political theory. He is also an extremely controversial figure for having worked in official appointments for the Nazi regime, including as author of legal studies defending Nazi racial policies, because of which he lost his academic post and retreated into virtual exile after the war. On the other hand, Schmitt was a Catholic and, since his death, the theological aspects of his work have gained increasing scholarly attention from theologians. And it is because of his work that the phrase 'political theology' resurfaced in the twentieth century and was seized upon by those at the forefront of the birth of a new discipline within academic theology.

There is no question that Schmitt's work has had a constructive influence on the political theology of the past century. His most famous dictum, 'All significant concepts of the modern theory of the state are secularized theological concepts',[6] has opened up possibilities for many avenues of political theology. For just one example, throughout the work of William Cavanaugh, and now well-represented by the several essays collected in the volume, *Migrations of the Holy*, there is an argument about how ideas of salvation, duty and devotion once reserved for God and the church migrated in the modern era to the nation state.[7] In other words, there did not actually arise a 'secular' state or sphere from which the marks of religious belief and devotion were absent, rather those marks were transposed and people began to look to the state as the giver of salvation and the body worthy of their deepest loyalty and devotion.

But there is also Schmitt's most infamous dictum, 'the political is the total'. Though some cite more innocent intentions for this statement,[8] it can obviously be interpreted as a brutal affirmation of naked political power, as in this example from a recent journal article:

> For Schmitt, then, politics as supreme power is the bedrock of all reality and consequently determines the truth of the world . . . In as much as this is the case for Schmitt could we not say that he was NOT in fact a thinker of political theology, but of the political (or power) altogether sundered from the theological?[9]

We will set Schmitt to one side for now, noting that the discussion of his significance continues, with some seeing him as the 'godfather' of political theology, and others seeing him as one of its most impeachable distorters.

The authors and groups introduced in this book are indisputably connected to and influential in political theology. However, it is important to understand that many of the theologians discussed here did not or do not refer to their own work as 'political theology'. For those historical figures before the twentieth century, the discipline and the label did not yet exist – nor would they have understood why the 'political' should be separated out from other theology in this sense. And many of those who have written theology since the mid-twentieth century (i.e. to whom the label was available) understand their work primarily in terms of doctrinal or systematic theology, or in terms of one of the disciplines we might describe as parallel discourses to political theology: Christian Ethics, Moral Theology and Catholic Social Teaching.

The labels are further confused and confusing because some theologians who do label their own work as a form of Political, Public or Liberation Theology – the different forms of contemporary political theology which will be introduced in Chapter 2 – would contest the claim that other theologians not explicitly doing such work should be included here. Some contend that theology which is not intentionally and explicitly 'political' is ideological instead, and/or that theology which is not intentionally and explicitly 'public' is sectarian instead (slightly more gracious is the term 'church theology'). D. Stephen Long (who has faced such critique) has argued that '[f]ew theologians these days would claim their work is "apolitical"', and that it is differing understandings of 'politics' and the 'public' which are at work, and which should be interpreted more charitably between fellow theologians.[10] We will also see in Chapter 2 that disputes about whether particular theologies are properly 'political' or 'public' often have to do with the tensions between the first and second generations of twentieth- and twenty-first-century schools of thought within the discipline.

A final distinction should be made: I am also excluding from this introduction 'civil religion' as a form of political theology. If political theology is defined even more broadly than the definition from Scott and Cavanaugh which I am assuming, it could encompass more instances of the intersection of theology and politics. Most important among these would likely be civil religion. This phenomena has mainly been studied by academics in relation to the American context, but is certainly relevant elsewhere. First introduced in the work of Jean-Jacques Rousseau (1712–78) and explored in depth in the twentieth century by Robert Bellah in particular,[11] civil religion is the set of beliefs, symbols and rituals which amount to a quasi-religion of the nation. Some sociologists and political theorists have described it in either neutral or positive terms as a force which draws the nation together and gives a sense of national transcendence, while Christian theologians have been more critical of civil religion as bastardized theology or even idolatry. However, in following Scott's and Cavanaugh's definition of political theology, civil religion is excluded as a *form of* political theology as it is neither intentionally analytic nor critical. However, it is not excluded as a *topic of* political theology because it is precisely the sort of phenomenon a political theologian might analyse and critique. In fact, it is one manifestation of the 'migration of the holy' explored by Cavanaugh.

This book will proceed in two parts. Part One is a further exploration of the definition of political theology. Chapter 1 explores the question, When did political theology emerge? We will see that in terms of Christian political theology (having already granted the roots of ancient political theology in Athens and Rome, and modern political theology in Schmitt as discussed above), this question can be answered in at least three ways: political theology begins in scripture, it begins with St Augustine's *City of God* and it begins in the twentieth century as a distinct theological discipline. Chapter 2 is something of a map to help readers who are new to political theology distinguish between the different ways in which the task of political theology is understood by its various practitioners, both historical and contemporary. I will introduce five sets of classifications which can help identify a given work of political theology in terms of historical, theological, ecclesial and academic trajectories.

Having established broadly what political theology is, when and how it emerged and how various theologians have conceived of its task, we move on to Part Two. Each of the chapters in Part Two is an introduction to a set of issues with which political theologians have engaged both in Christian history and in recent publications. In each chapter a brief overview of some of the central issues at stake for political theologians will be followed by introductions to a few specific theologians, groups or works of political theology which will demonstrate various approaches to some of the issues at stake. Each of these chapters is meant to be something of a tasting session for those who are new to the discipline; the chapters serve to briefly acquaint you with the questions that are on the table and just a few hints at how some theologians have answered some of those questions. Throughout the book, much of the work of introducing you to political theology is done in the endnotes. I have not used these only as a way of citing my own sources, but as extensive pointers towards the next level of reading on each topic, issue, theologian and school of thought.

What I hope to accomplish through the combination of the map of the terrain offered in Part One along with the tasting sessions offered in Part Two and the road signs to the next level offered in the endnotes – if you will forgive this hopeless mixture of metaphors – is to give readers confidence to embark upon further reading in the field, further discussion with fellow students, colleagues and church members, and – most of all – further and more thoughtful engagement between the theological and the political in their own lives and communities.

PART ONE

DEFINING POLITICAL THEOLOGY

CHAPTER 1

THE EMERGENCE OF POLITICAL THEOLOGY

There are at least three different ways to describe how and when political theology came into existence. In the first instance, many theologians would want to point to the Jewish and Christian scriptures as beginning the project of political theology. The political significance of Israel, Jesus and the church are inseparable from their spiritual and historical significance in scripture. If asked to name the first and most significant post-biblical work of political theology, many theologians would cite Augustine's *De Civitate Dei (City of God)* as the seminal text. Many consider the post-biblical project of political theology to have begun there. And while in one sense Christian theologians have been engaging in political theology continuously since Augustine, it is also important to note the emergence of political theology as a distinct academic discipline in the mid-to-late twentieth century. There are specific reasons why political theology became its own field of study within the last two generations of Christian theologians. In this chapter we will explore each of these moments of emergence of political theology.

SCRIPTURE AND POLITICAL THEOLOGY

Some political theologians are particularly attentive to scripture as containing works of political theology and setting out the task of theological reflection upon the political. Scripture can be described as both the original work of and the on-going primary source for Christian political theology. Walter Brueggemann describes how inseparable politics and theology are in the scriptures' narratives of Israel.

> [T]he self-presentation of Israel in song and story is inescapably a *theological politics* in which the defining presence of YHWH, the God of Israel, impinges upon every facet of the political; or conversely, Israel's self-presentation is inescapably a *political theology* in which YHWH, the God of Israel, is intensely engaged with questions of power and with policies and practices that variously concern the distribution of goods and access. In Israel's self-presentation, there is no politics not theologically marked, no theology not politically inclined.[1]

However, in political theology as in all theological disciplines, one does well to note from the outset that the scriptures speak with more than one voice. Brueggemann proposes that one could 'draw up a grid that suggests that certain kinds of literature perform certain political functions': Torah performs a paradigmatic function – it sets the pattern, parameters and framework for politics – while the prophets perform the confrontational function of seeking enactment of the paradigm in concrete circumstances – they confront the powers-that-be and hold them to account in relation to Torah.[2] This grid could be extended, of course, to include New Testament literature. Christopher Rowland sees a strand of uncompromising countercultural politics in the synoptic Gospels, James and Revelation alongside a certain degree of political accommodation in the Pauline letters.[3]

Two theologians in particular are known for their late-twentieth-century works of political theology arising primarily from scripture. We will look briefly at the work of each of these prominent political theologians in order to illustrate how it can be said that political theology begins in scripture, as well as to illustrate the key political features of the Bible. These include especially the political shape and significance of Israel; the relationship between the monarchs and the prophets; the meaning of the kingdom of God and the sovereign reign of Jesus Christ, the relationship between Israel, Christ and the church; and the political shape and significance of the church in the time between the Christ-event and the coming kingdom.[4] The scriptural themes which have been most prominent in political theology include creation, liberation and exodus, sovereignty and kingship, peace and justice, diaspora and sojourning, salvation and redemption, church and empire, the end of time and the last things. Our introduction to the uses of scripture in the work of John Howard Yoder and Oliver O'Donovan will illustrate how two theologians have employed and interpreted some of these features and themes, as well as how profound differences continue to arise between those who share a basic agreement concerning the political significance of scripture.

JOHN HOWARD YODER (1927–97)

John Howard Yoder was a Mennonite theologian and Christian ethicist who spent much of his career as a professor at the University of Notre Dame. While he drew extensively on his own Anabaptist tradition, he also sought both to transform that tradition and to show other Christians the deeply 'catholic' aspects of it. Yoder's most well-known and widely read book, *The Politics of Jesus*,[5] argued that the New Testament depicts Jesus as a political figure, killed for political reasons, and the church as a political body gathered as a political witness. We will return to this argument in Chapter 4. Here I will consider Yoder's corpus as a whole, from which a clear argument about the political witness of scripture emerges.[6]

Though Yoder is best known for his work on the politics of Jesus and thus his treatment of the New Testament, his biblical work does not begin there. Continuity between the two testaments and between Judaism and Christianity was important to his political theology.[7] He argued that two opposing political impulses were exhibited in the life of Israel: the Davidic vision of a settled, landed kingdom under monarchy, and the prophetic/exilic vision of a sojourning, counter-witnessing people with no king but YHWH. Yoder believed that the internal judgement of scripture was that God intended and Israel was most faithfully herself in the latter, not the former. He called this stream 'Jeremianic' as opposed to Davidic, and he identifies it in texts such as Judges 9, 1 Samuel 8, Deuteronomy 17.14-20 and Jeremiah – texts which question the faithfulness of the Davidic kingdom or embrace the life of sojourning in exile. Particularly important is 1 Samuel 8, where the elders of Israel demand a king and Samuel is told solemnly to warn the people of the ills that will come upon them if they reject YHWH as king and demand a human king instead. Yoder noted the importance of the fact that this counter-witness was preserved in the canonization of Hebrew scripture. 'It is of great significance that, however the traditions now grouped in the Hebrew canon were remembered and then redacted, these texts kept alive the memory of how the rise of the Davidic dynasty had been a disappointment not only to Samuel but to God.'[8]

In the texts of the Babylonian captivity, Yoder noted the development of a narrative of diaspora as opportunity and even as normative. 'The move to Babylon was not a two-generation parenthesis, after which the Davidic or Solomonic project was supposed to take up again where it had left off. It was rather the beginning, under a firm, fresh prophetic mandate, of a new phase of the Mosaic project.'[9] Central to the life of Israel as a diaspora community is the conviction that the sovereignty of God is greater than the sovereignty of political rulers, thus the community of faith does not need to be in control of or aligned with political powers in order for God's will to be done in human history. The government is not 'the primary bearer of the movement of history'.[10]

According to Yoder, Jesus identified himself with the prophetic/exilic vision in opposition to the Davidic vision. However, Jesus did not refuse to assume the role of king by rejecting the prevailing, Davidic interpretation of the character of the coming king and kingdom. Instead, he identified himself with Isaiah's suffering servant, thus redefining kingship.[11] Nor was Jesus' rejection of Davidic kingship an embrace of apoliticism – a statement that his kingdom was 'spiritual' instead of political. Rather, it was a redefinition of what it means to rule. 'The alternative to how the kings of the earth rule is not "spirituality" but servanthood.'[12] Jesus' rejection of the standard account of kingship results in the people's rejection of Jesus,[13] and leads Jesus to the cross. 'It is evident in Jesus that when God comes to be King, Jesus rejects the sword and the throne, taking up instead the whip of cords and the cross.'[14] However, rejection and suffering do not lead to abdication of kingship or failure of Christ's kingdom. Instead, the cross most boldly and perfectly enacts kingship and kingdom, and by the cross Jesus ascends to a different throne. '[T]he cross is not defeat. Christ's obedience unto death was crowned by the miracle of the resurrection and the exaltation at the right hand of God.'[15]

The connection between Christ's suffering and his kingly exaltation is confirmed in a passage which Yoder treated in several places, the vision of the lamb in Revelation 4–5. In these chapters, John sees a vision of four creatures, twenty-four elders and myriad angels worshipping the lamb who was slain, the only one in heaven or on earth worthy to open the scroll with seven seals. Yoder described the scroll as containing the meaning of history, and it is *because* the lamb was slain that he is worthy to open the scroll, worthy of honour and worshipped by the multitudes. '[T]he cross and not the sword, suffering and not brute power determines the meaning of history.'[16] In fact, Yoder argued that the visions of Revelation do not repudiate the way of the cross, rather they provide another revelation that the cross is in fact God's way in this world. Revelation is 'about how the crucified Jesus is a more adequate key to understanding what God is about in the real world of empires and armies and markets than is the ruler in Rome, with all his supporting military, commercial, and sacerdotal networks'.[17] When Jesus returns and the kingdom is consummated, we will not see a Christ who has abandoned his cross. Rather, the 'consummation is first of all the vindication of the way of the cross'.[18]

The vision of the lamb in Revelation is important in Yoder's work for both Christological and ecclesiological reasons, and he returns to the vision often in descriptions of the significance of the church.[19] In the vision, John sees not only a slain lamb, but also a community gathered to worship the lamb. Persons from every tribe, nation and kingdom are gathered under the lordship of Christ to rule and reign with him.[20] This is a vision 'of the gathering of the church', and it is in the church 'where it is already clear that [Jesus] rules'.[21] The church is the space in which humans find the meaning of their history and where that meaning is enacted.

> [T]he meaning of history lies not in the acquisition and defense of the culture and the freedoms of the West, not in the aggrandizement of material comforts and political sovereignty, but in the calling together 'for God saints from every tribe and language and people and nation,' a 'people of his own who are zealous for good deeds.'[22]

However, the sovereignty of Christ is not manifest exclusively in the church. While the church is the present embodiment and anticipation of the ultimate triumph of God's redemption, and thus serves as the 'scaffolding' of history, the world, even in its rebellion, is ruled over by Christ.[23] By 'world' Yoder meant the realm of human existence in which Christ's lordship is not yet recognized, as distinguished from the realm where there is willing submission to Christ.[24] The world is not aware that Christ is sovereign, and the visible reign of Christ through the church does not look like sovereignty to the world because it is characterized by non-violence and servanthood. This is not to say that the church is apolitical, rather that the church rules with Christ insomuch as she rules through servanthood just as Christ revealed his kingship to be a redefinition of politics and power. The shape of human history between the two comings of Christ is determined by the fact that a visible community of Christ's reign is being gathered, even in the face of the invisibility of his sovereignty over all the powers. 'The fact that God extends Christ's reign in a hidden way through the powers and in a visible way through the servant church is the reason for history. This is why time goes on.'[25]

The church reigns with Christ not for her own aggrandizement but as beacon and foretaste of the kingdom way available to and meant for all creation. 'The people of God are not a substitute or an escape from the whole world's being brought to the effective knowledge of divine righteousness; the believing community is the beginning, the pilot run, the bridgehead of the new world on the way.'[26] The politics of the church are not separate from but do transcend normal human politics. 'Jesus made it clear that the nationalized hope of Israel had been a misunderstanding, and that God's true purpose was the creation of a new society, unidentifiable with any of the local, national, or ethnic solidarities of any time.'[27]

The church's transcendence of such solidarities and its distinctness from the 'world' were most radically compromised, according to Yoder, through Constantinianism, and this critique is central to his entire corpus.[28] While the phenomenon of Constantinianism is named for the emperor, Constantine, who issued the Edict of Toleration in 311, ending the Diocletian persecution of Christianity, Yoder's concern did not lie there: 'Our concern is not with Constantine the man . . . Nor do we suggest that the year 311 represented an immediate reversal without preparation or unfolding. . . he stands for a new era in the history of Christianity.'[29] In this new era which extended through the middle ages, Yoder argued, there were significant ecclesiological and theological shifts. The church had been a persecuted minority and became an established majority; eventually in Christian nations 'the church was everybody'.[30] The church had previously been a visible community ruled by Christ, while Christ's sovereignty over human history was an invisible hope awaiting the fullness of the kingdom to be established on earth, but in Constantinianism the true church became an invisible reality and the empire was understood as a visible sign of God's rule on earth. Where the people of God had been God's agent of social embodiment in the world, secular rulers were now understood as God's particular servants and the church moved into a role of 'chaplaincy' to their social agency.[31] All this paved the way for interiorization and spiritualization of formerly socially and politically embodied Christianity. In other words, in Constantinianism the sojourning, prophetic faithfulness of Israel and the redefinition of power and kingship enacted by Jesus, are both rejected in favour of standard arrangements of settlement and sovereignty. It would be easy to assume that Yoder's critique of Constantinianism would, in the contemporary context, be aimed at nations which retain established churches. However, for Yoder, the contemporary consequences of the ecclesial, theological and ethical shifts in Constantinianism are especially prominent and pernicious in new, neo-Constantinian forms in places like America where the institutions of church and state are officially separated.[32]

One of the biblical texts which might most often be cited in argument against views of biblical political theology such as Yoder's is Romans 13.1-7, which many have interpreted as aligning New Testament political theology with the more monarchical stream of the Old Testament, teaching that God ordains governments and commissions them to exercise violent force, and that Christian duty entails obedience to such authorities. First, Yoder questioned this interpretation of what God is said to do in relation to government. 'God is not said to *create* or *institute* or *ordain* the powers that be, but only to *order* them, to put them in order, sovereignly to tell them where they belong, what is their place.'[33] Yoder also questioned this interpretation of *obedience* as the required response. He interprets the text as directive for the particular circumstance of potential tax revolts within the Roman Empire; Paul is urging his readers not to revolt in this instance and warning them of the force they will encounter if they do. Key to Yoder's interpretation is the idea of *submission*. If one submits herself to the government this may mean obedience when it is justified, but in other cases 'submission must be in the form of disobedience and accepting punishment for it'. When the government acts as 'a sober and righteous instrument of order in society' as described in Romans 13, then the duty of submission is obedience as enjoined there.[34] However, the Bible clearly attests to the tendency of governments to rebel against God, especially in Revelation. Yoder called Romans 13 and Revelation 13 – where two beasts arise and demand the people's worship – representations of 'the two dimensions of the life of any state'.[35] To say that God can work through coercive governmental powers is not to say that God blesses the use of political violence by Christians; it is to say something more like the Old Testament attestations to God's use of the nations to punish Israel. 'This takes place, however, without his declaring that such destructive action by pagan powers which he thus uses is morally good or that participation in it is incumbent upon his covenant people.'[36]

In summary, we see in Yoder's interpretation of the political theology of the scriptures a counter-politics of the gathered, believing community of God's people which is marked by visible faithfulness to God's sovereignty instead of grasping for political power, and which redefines politics through the cruciform shape of a church practicing non-violent servant leadership in response to the life and teachings of Jesus and in anticipation of his coming kingdom.

OLIVER O'DONOVAN

Oliver O'Donovan is a contemporary political theologian and Christian ethicist. He is an Anglican and a professor in the University of Edinburgh. His work has been described as an attempt to 're-state an Augustinian-Reformed approach to Church-state relations and distinguish this approach from political theologies that draw on the Aristotelian-Thomistic tradition, the Anabaptist/Radical Reformation tradition and more modern schools, notably Liberation Theology and liberal Protestantism'.[37] Each of these traditions and schools of thought will be introduced in Chapter 2. For now we will explore

O'Donovan's use of scripture as a political text, which is shown most clearly in *The Desire of the Nations*, which has also been called 'the manifesto' of his project of political theology.[38]

We see in *The Desire of the Nations* that O'Donovan agrees with Yoder that scripture witnesses to a political theology through a clear trajectory traceable through the two testaments of the Christian scriptures. Christian political theology begins with Israel and 'the governing principle is the kingly rule of God, expressed in Israel's corporate existence and brought to final effect in the life, death and resurrection of Jesus'.[39] However, where Yoder finds that this witness calls the monarchy into question and makes the sojourning, kingless Israel normative, O'Donovan finds a very different political theology. He argues that we must not construct a 'subversive counter-history' but must rely on the 'official history of Israel'.[40] On O'Donovan's interpretation, this 'official history' begins with YHWH as king and then moves to the divinely ordained monarchy in which the king functioned as YHWH's representative. 'Even the narrative of 1 Samuel 8 is in fact an apologia for the monarchy addressed to its natural antagonists; it intends to leave no doubt that the monarchy came to existence by YHWH's decision.'[41] For O'Donovan, the prophetic tradition was one of holding monarchs accountable to the divine law; it does not call into question the divinely given mandate of the monarchy. Yoder noted how remarkable and important it was that a counter-history of the monarchy was kept within the canon, and that it served as scripture's own internal judgement against the Davidic vision. O'Donovan, however, considers attempts to draw normativity from counter-history a failure to accept Israel's 'official' history.

O'Donovan accepts that the experience of Israel in the Babylonian captivity 'became the paradigm of Jewish existence thereafter',[42] however, it is paradigmatic for O'Donovan not in a morally normative way, as it was for Yoder who claimed the normativity of landless Israel with only YHWH for king. Captivity for O'Donovan is paradigmatic in a descriptive way: this would be the way of life from now on, as even return to the land was not a restoration of the monarchy. The paradigm shift in the captivity was that of 'dual authority': while Israel continued to live under the authority of YHWH, they now also had to live under the authority of foreign rulers. In the post-exilic era, this duality continued; though the Temple was restored the monarchy was not.

Yoder and O'Donovan agree that Jesus' declaration of the coming of the kingdom was politically significant. However, Yoder saw Jesus as a king who redefined kingship, rejecting the Davidic interpretation and decisively aligning Christian political theology with suffering service instead of the exercise of violent power, while O'Donovan argues that 'Jesus laid claim to the legacy of Davidic expectation in his great entry into Jerusalem'.[43] O'Donovan acknowledges that this legacy was 'an ambiguous one', that 'Jesus would neither endorse nor reject everything that could be inferred from it',[44] and that Jesus preferred to identify himself with a different figure of sovereignty and power, the 'Son of Man' from Daniel 7 (whereas Yoder emphasizes Jesus preferring to identify himself with Isaiah's suffering servant). Nevertheless, for O'Donovan, Jesus has taken up the role of monarch as attested to in Israel's 'official' history.

More significant for O'Donovan than Jesus' alignment with Davidic monarchy, however, is the change in 'dual authority' (or 'the doctrine of the two' or the 'two cities' or 'two kingdoms', as this shifting reality is variously called throughout the book). Israel had once lived under the singular authority of YHWH as divine ruler as represented through the monarch, until the shift to dual authority in the exile and post-exilic era. When Jesus was risen and exalted, the 'Two Kingdoms period, in which Temple without power and praetorium without worship coexisted in some kind of parallel, was declared closed'.[45] And yet this 'triumph of the kingdom' was not yet fully realized. In the Christ-event, 'the duality inherited from Israel's past underwent a transformation. The Two Cities, with their concomitant Two Rules expressing Israel's alienation from its calling, gave way to the Two Eras. The coming era of God's rule held the passing era in suspension'.[46] While all political authorities 'have been made subject to God's sovereignty in the Exaltation of Christ', this assertion is qualified by O'Donovan with a second: 'this awaits a final universal presence of Christ to become fully apparent.'[47]

Because the subjection of all authorities to God through Christ is not yet 'fully apparent', according to O'Donovan, just as the political theologian must be wary of constructing counter-histories from within the Old Testament, when moving to the New Testament we must also be wary of constructing political theologies from narrow 'Jesuology'. What is necessary is a broader conception of how the kingdom of God, exhibited in YHWH's divine kingship and in the monarchy of Israel is also manifest in the advent, passion, resurrection and ascension of Jesus Christ – not the attempt to derive political theology narrowly from Jesus' life and teachings.

> In the end every political Jesuology offers a helpful illusion: let us model ourselves on Jesus, ignoring Caiaphas and Pilate, then we will at least achieve something, even if it is not what we hope to achieve . . . A secure political theology must base itself on 'the hidden counsel of God' which worked also through Caiaphas and Pilate.[48]

O'Donovan explicitly rejects Yoder's reading of Romans 13 and asserts instead that of central importance to its reading is 'the authority which remains to secular government in the aftermath of Christ's triumph'.[49] Having been overcome but not yet removed, what authority do human governments now exercise? Where Yoder describes their continued relevance in terms of ordering common life, O'Donovan describes it in terms of judgement, as symbolized by 'the sword' in Romans 13. '[S]ecular authorities are no longer in the fullest sense mediators of the rule of God,' as they had been in Israel's monarchy, but they now 'mediate his judgments only'.[50]

O'Donovan echoes Yoder when he describes the vision of Revelation 4, summarizing the opening of the sealed scroll: 'Jesus' death and resurrection are the key to history'.[51] However, while Yoder interpreted this key as relating to suffering service as the nature of Christ's reign and the drawing together of a set-apart people in the church, O'Donovan interprets it in terms of cycles of human sin and divine judgement described in the subsequent visions. O'Donovan agrees with Yoder in asserting 'the true character of the church as a political society' ruled by Christ alone, and that it should not be 'accommodated to existing political societies as a system of religious practice that can flourish within them, a kind of service-agency (inevitably clerical) which puts itself at the disposal of a multitude of rulers' – precisely what Yoder calls 'chaplaincy'.[52] However, he goes on to radically disagree with Yoder when he argues that the church's 'essential nature as a governed society' – a political society governed by Christ – 'is hidden, to be discerned by faith as the ascended Christ who governs it is to be discerned by faith'.[53] For Yoder, such a view is a tragic consequence of Constantinianism; the rule of Christ should be most visible precisely in the life and politics of the church, while it remains largely hidden in the rest of society and the politics of human government.

O'Donovan disagrees because he does not believe Christ's reign over all authorities is necessarily, or has been historically, hidden. For him, the great strength of Christendom was precisely this: its acknowledgement that secular powers were in subjection to Christ. In O'Donovan's account, 'the core idea of Christendom' was that 'the rulers of the world have bowed before Christ's throne'.[54] Where Yoder saw something going very wrong in the church as Rome came to greater toleration of Christianity, O'Donovan insists of the Edict of Milan (Constantine's official toleration of Christianity in 313), 'There is no point in regretting this. The church of that age had to do contextual theology just as we do . . . This was the logical conclusion of their confidence in mission, the confirmation of what they had always predicted.'[55] Thus, for O'Donovan, an appropriately understood and enacted Christendom arrangement is the most faithful way to embody the political tradition he has traced through the histories of Israel and the Christ-event. While Yoder steadfastly refused to identify biblical political theology with any particular modern political form, O'Donovan concluded that 'a Christian theologian can venture to characterise a normative political culture broadly in continuity with the Western liberal tradition' which he identifies with early-modern Christendom.[56]

Yoder and O'Donovan share much in common, and as we will see, can in one sense be considered as members of the same school of thought within political theology.[57] They agree that biblical political theology begins with Israel, that a distinctly Jewish political trajectory is both embraced and redefined by Jesus and the Christ-event, and that the church is a distinct political community and witness to the coming kingdom which he inaugurated but which is not yet fully realized. One finds several statements in each of their works which either could have written. Most striking is the following from O'Donovan.

> The church does not philosophise about a future world; it demonstrates the working of the coming kingdom within this one. Through the authorisation of the Holy Spirit it squares up to civil authority and confronts it. This may lead to martyrdom, or to mutual service.[58]

However, they also have some striking differences. They part company primarily on whether this witness to the coming kingdom and squaring up to civil authority can be done faithfully within an arrangement like Christendom. Their differing conclusions on that matter result from at least two key differences which we have seen above: they hold up two different streams of thought from within the Old Testament as normative for both Israel and the church, and they locate the significance for the church of the 'not yet' of the kingdom of God differently. O'Donovan finds political normativity in the stream which affirms Israel's monarchy, and he locates the significance of the 'not yet' in the hiddenness of the fullness of Christ's reign over the church. Yoder finds political normativity in the prophetic and exilic stream, and he locates the significance of the 'not yet' in the hiddenness of Christ's reign over all that which exists apart from the church. Critics of Yoder often ask, 'Where is this church you speak of?', wondering when and where the church has existed which is the social and political embodiment of the 'already' of the visible reign of Christ. Perhaps the question should also be posed to O'Donovan, 'Where is this Christendom you speak of?', noting that there is at least as much – if not more – difficulty in identifying actual times and places where political rule has been a clear embodiment of the 'already' of the powers' subjection to Christ.

AUGUSTINE AND THE TWO CITIES

Apart from the scriptures themselves – which should be regarded as the seminal texts of all branches of theology – most would identify Augustine's *De Civitate Dei (City of God)* as the founding text of political theology.

Augustine's political theology was formed in the context of the changing status of the Roman Empire as well as the church's relation to the empire, both of which were shifting dramatically during his lifetime. Rome was sacked in 410 and the empire was in clear decline; it would fall entirely by 480. Augustine began writing *De Civitate Dei* in 413 and completed it 13 years later. His purposes were apologetic, theological and pastoral. His apologetic purpose was to convince non-Christians that the fall of Rome and the disintegration of the empire was not the fault of Christianity. This included a critique of Rome's morality and theology, suggesting that these were shadows of what is true. Augustine was calling Romans not only to stop blaming Christianity, but to recognize how Christianity could answer questions which the virtues of the Roman intellectual tradition and the polytheism of Roman paganism could not answer.

Among his theological and pastoral purposes was the making of a new argument for Christians about their relationship to the empire. Many saw the Roman Empire and its official recognition of Christianity as the clear sign of God working in human history; for them, the decline of the empire would have felt like the literal end of history or at least a cause to seriously reconsider this view of God's sovereignty. Augustine wanted to reassure Christians that God indeed had been working and would continue to work in human history, but that powers like the Roman Empire were not ultimate. According to Augustine, human government is required to restrain sinfulness in the ordering of common life, but it cannot establish true peace or true justice. Christians are sojourners in this world. They make use of all the earthly goods available, but for eternal purposes. They work together for earthly justice and peace, all the while knowing that true and absolute justice and peace can only be established by God. The Christian faith points backward to see God's work in salvation history, and points forward to the *eschaton* when God's purposes will finally be consummated and complete. And it is in light of both these realities that Christians currently live and seek to order their common life.

Augustine made this argument through a description of two cities: the city of God and the earthly city. Many have confused the two cities as representing 'church and state'. This is inaccurate for several reasons. First, the entity of the 'state' as we know it did not come into existence until the modern era; even if Augustine were writing about the church and x, x would be empire instead of state. However, even with this correction, 'church and empire' would be an equally inaccurate description of the two cities. As Rowan Williams has noted of *City of God*, 'We should look less for a systematic account of "church" and "world" (let alone church and state), more for a scheme for reflecting on the nature of social virtue . . . The opposition is not between public and private, church and world, but between political virtue and political vice'.[59]

The two cities can also easily be misunderstood as highly the-
oretical or conceptual categories, but Augustine's description of
them is intensely concrete and historical. Augustine traced the
history of the two cities through the entire biblical canon, from
Cain and Abel, through Noah and the flood, through the Hebrews
in Egypt, through the history of Israel, to Christ and the church.
Through this narrative, Augustine described the city of God as
created by the love of God, founded in peace and always ultimately
orientated towards loving God. This city is populated by all those
who worship God, in both heaven and earth. This heavenly city –
not to be confused with Heaven, or a future and other-worldly
reality – is currently sojourning in this world, but will continue to
exist when this world is no longer. Within this city true justice and
true peace are possible, and the citizens serve one another in love.
Their emotions and desires are rightly ordered; they see their bodies, souls, virtues and pleasures as goods insofar as they serve the
purposes of God. And they make use of all the goods of the earth,
knowing them as true goods, but only for God's sake.

By contrast, the earthly city was created by self-love, founded
in violence, is orientated towards and glories in itself. The earthly
city is at home in this world and will cease to exist when this world
ends. Temporal, limited forms of peace and justice are pursued
in this city, but its polity is also characterized by the domination
of the powerful who assert their own strength and subjugate all
others. Emotions and desires disturb the earthly city because they
are disordered due to not finding their end in God. Bodies, souls,
virtues and pleasures are taken to be goods in their own right, as
are all earthly goods.

These two cities are interwoven and intermixed within and
throughout human history. Only in the *eschaton* will the earthly
city pass away and the city of God exist unmingled, no longer
sojourning in the world. Two key passages from Augustine summarize his presentations of the two cities:

> We see then that the two cities were created by two kinds of love:
> the earthly city was created by self-love reaching the point of
> contempt for God, the Heavenly City by the love of God carried
> as far as contempt of self. In fact, the earthly city glories in itself,
> the Heavenly City glories in the Lord. The former looks for glory
> from men, the latter finds its highest glory in God, the witness

of a good conscience. The earthly lifts up its head in its own glory, the Heavenly City says to its God: 'My glory; you lift up my head.' In the former, the lust for domination lords it over its princes as over the nations it subjugates; in the other both those put in authority and those subject to them serve one another in love, the rulers by their counsel, the subjects by obedience. The one city loves its own strength shown in its powerful leaders; the other says to its God, 'I will love you, my Lord, my strength.'[60]

Nevertheless, both cities alike enjoy the good things, or are afflicted with the adversities of this temporal state, but with a different faith, a different expectation, a different love, until they are separated by the final judgement, and each receives her own end, of which there is no end.[61]

Augustine did not identify the empire with the kingdom of God; his description of the earthly city very clearly involves a critique of Rome and an argument that such polities can never be truly just because they are not rightly orientated.[62] However, Augustine was also not using the concept of the earthly city to carve out a separate 'secular' space in which human government can operate legitimately without regard for the 'sacred' which is the purview of the church.[63] In fact, it is important to note that Augustine, like most premodern authors, used the term 'secular' not to mean that which is not 'sacred', but to mean that which is temporal and not eternal. As William Cavanaugh has argued, identifying Augustine with an argument for a secular, non-sacred sphere of society neglects the fact that there are two distinct (yet intermingled) cities in Augustine, 'not one society in which there is a division of labor'.[64] In fact, Cavanaugh's clarification on this point merits quoting at length:

Augustine has no theory of church and state, no spatial carving up of one society into spheres of influence. There is no sense that there is a single given public square in which the church must find its place. Augustine complexifies space by arguing that the church itself is a kind of public; indeed it is the most fully public community. The city of God has to do with ordering matters that are considered public, because the city of God makes use of the same temporal goods as the earthly city, but in different ways and for different ends. There is no division between earthly goods and heavenly goods, secular and sacred; there is no sphere of activities that are the peculiar responsibility of the earthly city. The city of God, therefore, is not part of a larger whole, but is a public in its own right. Indeed, the city of God is the only true 'public thing' according to Augustine, as pagan Roman rule had failed to be a *res publica* by refusing to enact justice and serve God.[65]

Within this narrative of two cities are also found marks of theological encounters which were part of Augustine's life story. As a young adult, he was an adherent of Manichaeism until his conversion which was aided by the preaching of St Ambrose of Milan. He soon became the bishop of Hippo at a time when there were more Donatists in Hippo than orthodox Catholics. These encounters with Manichaeism and Donatism were formative influences on Augustine's theology in general, including his political theology.

Manichaeism was named for the teachings of Mani, a third century Babylonian who believed that human beings were created by God as essentially spiritual and rational beings, and that they were trapped in physical bodies by an evil deity. Thus the physical body and world were hindrances to true human existence, and good and evil were equal metaphysical realities. Augustine's doctrine of original sin can be seen as a corrective to his previous Manichaeism, as it both affirms the goodness of creation while also seeking to explain the presence of evil within it. It is also important for Augustine that good and evil are not equal realities or forces; instead evil is essentially human turning away from delight in God to seek delight elsewhere. Evil has no independent existence; rather it is a privation of good. This also becomes important in his description of the two cities, where we see evil as a temporary reality originating in the human will, and that while sociality is part of created human nature, the need for coercive politics and government structures only exists as a result of the fall.

Donatism was named for the bishop Donatus, who was a proponent of a view which caused schism in the North African churches. There was a debate over the status of bishops who had collaborated with the empire during the Great Persecution of Diocletian (303–05). The Donatists believed that the church must be pure and holy, set apart from the world. For this reason they concluded that the sacraments administered by the offending bishops were not only ineffectual but also contaminating, besmirching the spot-less bride of Christ. Thus, they rebaptized converts to their cause. Augustine's opposition to this movement becomes apparent in *De Civitate Dei*, where the church is described as a mixed body of faithful and unfaithful members, and the earthly and heavenly cit-ies are inextricably intertwined on earth until the *eschaton*; the wheat cannot yet be separated from the tares.

Thus, in this seminal text of political theology we find already many of the issues we will see contemporary theologians struggling with below: the relationship between the church and the political, the role of Christ in that relationship, violence and peace, justice, creation and eschatology. These remain within the set of perennial concerns of Christian political theology, and *City of God* contin-ues to be recognized as the piece of work in which political theol-ogy most clearly and significantly emerged after the close of the biblical canon.

THE TWENTIETH CENTURY AND A DISTINCT DISCIPLINE

While Christian political theology is present already in scripture and has been included in the work of the church's theologians at least since St Augustine, political theology did not emerge as a dis-tinct discipline until the mid-to-late-twentieth century. There were several reasons for its emergence at this time.

It was in the 1960s that scholars in several disciplines began to come to terms with the fact that the removal of Christianity as a central feature of Western society was neither inevitable nor necessarily desirable; the thesis of secularization began to col-lapse. The thesis was that all modern, industrialized nations would become increasingly secularized: religious groups would continue to decrease in membership and the public workings of state and society would be increasingly free from religious influence. In the modern West, the Enlightenment deeply instilled in the conscious-ness of the academy and the populace alike the conviction that peo-ple and political processes and structures cannot be free nor ensure freedom if they are in any way beholden to or arising from theolog-ical convictions, practices or powers. The separation of theology and 'religion' from politics and government was seen as the chief necessity and crowning achievement of modernity, and secularization was sure to spread across the globe as nations modernized.[66] However, by the mid-twentieth century, honest and attentive sociologists, political theorists and philosophers as well as theologians began to interrogate the cluster of convictions surrounding modern secularization. Was the separation of politics and theology necessary and/or inevitable, or might things have happened differently? Is secularization spreading across the globe, or is it a European peculiarity? Has politics actually lost something of its own integrity and intelligibility without theology? For theologians, a further set of questions was raised: Has the separation of politics and theology been detrimental to theology as well as politics? Has the life and work of the Christian churches been inadequate because of this separation?

It is important to note here that the separation of church and state is a related and overlapping issue, but is not identical or to be confused with the question of theology and the political. As we have already seen in Yoder and O'Donovan, the work of political theology is done both by those deeply committed to the separation of church and state as well as those who favour establishment.

At the same time that the secularization thesis began to unravel, Western societies were undergoing radical social transformations and the Christian churches of the West were undergoing serious re-evaluations of their relationships with the modern world. These conversations became official in the Second Vatican Council of the Roman Catholic Church (1962–65), the World Council of Churches Conference on Church and Society in Geneva (1966) and the World Council of Churches Fourth Assembly in Uppsala (1968).

Both leading to and following from these conversations and shifts was the beginning of mid-twentieth-century political theology. In several different parts of the world, theologians began to insist that the political lay at the very centre of the Christian scriptures, the life and death of Jesus Christ, the Christian gospel and the Christian way of life. They were disturbed by how the spiritualization and privatization of Christianity had rendered their churches apathetic or impotent in the face of serious societal problems or changes. German theologians struggled to understand how the Holocaust could have occurred in their land and why so few Christians were willing and able to resist the Third Reich. Latin

American theologians and bishops became convinced that the gospel should be transforming the lives of the poor and challenging the societies which were perpetuating the mechanisms of poverty. Black and female theologians in North America began to question the ways in which the churches were complicit in the racism and sexism of society. And other North American theologians began to mourn a lack of public moral consensus and public space for Christian convictions. Collectively, these rising voices marked the beginning of political theology as a distinct theological discipline.

In Chapter 2 we will look more closely at each of these points of emergence, as well as other ways of characterizing differing forms of political theology both in historical theology and in the contemporary theological discipline.

CHAPTER 2

APPROACHES TO POLITICAL THEOLOGY

The reader who is new to the discipline of political theology may find herself encountering a wide variety of texts and conversations which go under the heading 'political theology' but which do not seem to be doing the same thing. This can make becoming familiar with the discipline perplexing indeed! In order to become conversant with the discipline, it is important to be aware of the different types of scholarship which are included within our working definition of political theology but which may begin with very different assumptions, draw on very different sources and aim towards very different goals.

There are at least four ways of distinguishing variations between approaches to political theology. The first is related to theological understandings of creation, fall and human nature. Some suggest that there are basically two types of political theology: one type begins from positive possibilities inherent in God's creation and the other type begins from human limitations due to sin. A second way would be to describe distinctive approaches to political theology according to theological traditions, noting the differences between Catholic, Lutheran, Reformed, Anglican, Anabaptist and Eastern Orthodox political theologies. Third, we can note differences between political theologies by contrasting three distinct approaches within twentieth-century scholarship:

Political Theology, Public Theology and Liberation Theology. Finally, it is also important to note more recently emerging schools of thought – what might be considered the second generation of political theologies.

As with any such scheme of categorization or typology, readers should be alert to the fact that while such structures serve the helpful purpose of making a wide variety of diverse information more readily digestible, they also are always and necessarily oversimplifications. The generalizations made below regarding movements or schools of thought cannot apply without exception to every thinker within that category, nor are the characteristics discussed or the movements and schools of thought themselves comprehensive. I offer these categories as *ways in* to understanding the field, not as ways of foreclosing further exploration of the field which will most certainly problematize them.

OPTIMISM VERSUS PESSMISIM OR COVENANT VERSUS LEVIATHAN

The first of these ways of differentiating approaches has the virtue of clear simplicity. It suggests there are basically two camps in political theology and all work on the subject arises from one perspective or the other. This is often described in terms of 'optimism' versus 'pessimism' or 'positive anthropology' versus 'negative anthropology'. On this view, political theologies are said to either be optimistic about what humans and human governments are capable of, or pessimistic about the limitations of sinful humanity.

One source of this difference can be in differing interpretations of and attitudes towards what the New Testament refers to as 'the principalities and powers'. If this concept is interpreted as a theology of government and social structures, these can be identified entirely with demonic or at least unredeemed social realities, as New Testament authors write in several places of Jesus Christ conquering and defeating these powers. Walter Wink has argued that this New Testament language refers to both the spiritual and material realities of social systems and structures, and that they are viewed both as part of God's good creation and as fallen and in need of redemption.[1]

Another source of 'optimism' and 'pessimism' in political theology is in readings of two of the Christian tradition's most influential political theologians: St Thomas Aquinas and St Augustine are often claimed as the patron saints of these two camps, respectively. Thomistic political theologies share Thomas's faith in the goodness of the created order and his conviction that God intends human government to contribute to human flourishing – to seek the common good. Augustinian political theologies, by contrast, are marked by the conviction that the fallen condition of humanity so significantly obscures the goodness of the original created order that we cannot expect so much from one another or from human institutions. On this view, human government as it exists was not part of God's original intentions for the ordering of human life or provision for the common good, instead it became necessary because of the fall and is required for the restraint and limitation of the sinfulness of our interrelations. The standard account of this difference between Aquinas and Augustine is often prone to overstatement or misreadings of their theologies. This can be seen, for example, in the introduction to a collection of the 'political writings' of Aquinas:

For St Augustine and those who wrote under his inspiration, earthly politics is on the whole a regrettable and squalid business. At best, it is a necessary evil. Political arrangements are inseparable from the sinful condition of fallen man. Government would not have come into existence at all had the Fall not occurred . . . Its redeeming feature is that it functions to limit and control man's destructive impulses, to punish the sinful and test the faith of the righteous . . . The 'recovery' of Aristotle equips St Thomas to forge a new kind of political theory: a political theory which we may characterise as milder and more optimistic precisely because it lacks Augustine's stringent insistence on the unworthiness of this world and its ends . . . Augustine, with his eyes fastened upon the world to come – the transcendent other world of the Christian Platonist – had found the present world unnatural, sin-laden, destructive and disordered, and its politics harsh and coercive merely . . . [Thomistic government] is not 'Augustinian' government. It is not ordained to do little more than hold the lid on human destructiveness by force and fear. It is a benevolent administration suited to the kind of sociable and co-operating creature that man is by nature . . . The purpose of secular government is not suppression and punishment, but the achievement of earthly wellbeing.[2]

It should already be evident from the brief introduction to Augustine's two cities in Chapter 1 that his 'pessimism' is overstated here, especially when it is attributed to him that the world, its government or its goods are 'necessary evil' or 'unworthy'. Likewise, some would contest the idea that Augustine's political theology limits the task of government to merely 'holding the lid on human destructiveness'. It is also the case that not all readings of Aquinas sit easily with 'optimism' as the central feature of his view of government. This 'optimism' is sometimes taken to be a naïve confidence in governments' ability to do good – as if sin has no negative consequences for politics – and an equally naïve confidence in human ability to know the good – as if sin has no negative consequences for human reason. Reading Aquinas reveals much more nuance. It is a very different thing to argue that the ordering of human society through the rule of some by others is an intended property of creation than to argue that all human government is good. It is a very different thing to argue that governments are intended by God to serve positive functions, to promote human flourishing and the common good, than to argue that governments will always do so. And it is a very different thing to argue that an inclination towards the good and against evil is part of human nature and that specific principles of this inclination can be discerned through human reason, than to argue that humans always perform these acts of discernment (to say nothing of application) appropriately. In every case, Aquinas argues the former rather than the latter.[3]

Several chapters of his longest written piece on human government, *De regimine principum* ('On the Government of Princes', also commonly known as *De regno*, 'On Kingship'), are dedicated to the ways in which every form of government can and often does go very wrong; he was well aware of the risks of human sinfulness: 'Peril lurks on either side, therefore: either the best form of government, kingship, may be shunned because tyranny is feared, or, if the risk is considered worthwhile, royal power may change into wicked tyranny.'[4] Aquinas considers at length how to avoid tyrannical rulers and what to do if they become tyrants, and he makes provision for the limitation of the power of monarchs and for resistance against tyrants and imposters (though he describes these in different terms in different places); his is not an unqualified argument for the goodness of or duty of subservience to power-as-it-exists.

Central to Thomas's political theology are two guiding features of his work in general: his effort to reason together with Aristotle, and the centrality of scripture and the theology of the church. A large number of the works of Aristotle became increasingly unknown in the West after the fall of the Roman Empire until they were rediscovered in the late twelfth and early thirteenth centuries. Aquinas was the first Christian theologian to systematically incorporate Aristotelianism into his philosophy. This 'synthesis', as it is so often called, shaped the work of Aquinas in many ways, but for our purposes it is most important to note two. First, Aristotle's moral philosophy was teleological; it was concerned with the *telos* of all things, with goals, ends and ultimate purposes. Thomas taught that the *telos* of human government is the common good, and that tyranny arises when the *telos* becomes the private good of those in power.[5] His definition of governing was 'to guide what is governed in a suitable fashion to its proper end'.[6] Second, Aristotle claimed that humans were by nature political animals.[7] Thomas took up Aristotle's maxim ('man is by nature a political animal') in *De regno*, noting that humans differ from other animals in that they are social and political animals, needing to live in community.[8] Aristotelian teleology and the claim that humans are inherently social and political come together theologically for Thomas. As Frederick Christian Bauerschmidt has noted,

> For human beings to flourish as human beings, they need some sort of structured way of living and flourishing *together*. This flourishing together is based on what Thomas calls 'the common good.' This is neither the aggregate of all individual goods, nor those goods that a given group of individuals happen to have in common. Rather, it is *God* who is the common good of all creatures, both as the source of all created goods, and as the end toward which they are drawn.[9]

Indeed, to highlight the Aristotelian features of Thomas's political thought is not to agree with the widely held view that Thomas was essentially an Aristotelian philosopher. Aquinas was first and foremost a theologian. Naming him as an Aristotelian can obscure the absolute centrality of scripture and the theological tradition (especially Augustine) as sources for his thought.

One of the key aspects of his thought which is cited in relation to political theology is his work on natural law. Many theologians are now alerting us to the fact that Thomas's doctrine of natural law has been received through centuries of shifts in Thomism specifically and natural law theory generally, and that one consequence of these shifts is an understanding of natural law as functioning independently from divine revelation. Natural law has been taken up by some as a means through which government and politics might be ordered in reference to universals available to every rational individual. This was not the case for Thomas.[10] In the *Summa Theologiae*[11] we see that the natural law (to which all humans have access through reason) is inextricably bound up with eternal law (God's governance over all creation) and divine law (that which has been revealed), and cannot be translated into human law without reference to them. In fact, natural law 'is nothing else than the rational creature's participation in the eternal law'.[12] Those who suspect that Thomistic notions of the common good and natural law are dependent upon unwarranted optimism in human nature do well to remember the dependence of the natural upon the divine which permeates the work of Aquinas. While through nature alone we may be inclined towards the good and able to establish that God exists, we cannot know who God is or precisely how we ought to order our common lives apart from divine revelation and the divine life: 'nature is crowned by grace'.

It should be clear now that an overstated pessimism-versus-optimism contrast between Augustine and Aquinas is generally inaccurate and unhelpful. However, one central aspect of the contrast between the two does hold: Augustine does consider government to be a necessity due to the fall, while Aquinas considers government to be an inherent feature of God's created order and human nature created in God's image. Augustine taught that God 'did not wish the rational being, made in his own image, to have dominion over any but irrational creatures, not man over man, but man over the beasts'.[13] Aquinas taught that only some types of dominion are the result of sin, such as the master–slave relationship, but by contrast, some have dominion over others which consists in leading them towards the common good. '[M]an is by nature a social animal, and so in the state of innocence would have lived a social life. But there cannot be social life among a multitude of people save under the direction of someone who is to look to the common good.'[14] Thus, according to Aquinas, there would have been some form of human government apart from the fall, and the ordering of human society is necessary because of the sociality of our created human nature, not our fallen sinfulness alone.

Jürgen Moltmann has described a related distinction not in terms of Aquinas and Augustine but of 'covenant' and 'Leviathan'. He associated 'covenant' with Calvinist federalism, central to which was the idea that in the establishment of governments, humans enter into covenant with one another which is related but subordinate to their covenant with God. For Moltmann, it is crucial that this theory of government is both based in trust – God's trust in human ability to form such a covenant, and trust of humans in one another – and is open to the people resisting tyrannical governments because their authority does not supersede that of the covenant with God. In the 'covenant' view, the state is a phenomenon of our created human nature, which is darkened by sin but which also is caught up in anticipation of the coming Kingdom of God. By contrast, Moltmann describes the 'Leviathan' of Thomas Hobbes, and latterly of Carl Schmitt, as based in the 'war of all against all' instead of trust, and in a contract of self-determination instead of a covenant of mutual fidelity. In the 'Leviathan' view, the state is 'a phenomenon of sin'.[15]

Many would suggest that the distinction between government having been intended by God as part of the goodness of creation and government being required only after the fall due to sin is a distinction which can appropriately exist within Christian political theologies. However, when the more 'pessimistic' view is taken up not only through Augustine (and possibly Luther) but also through Hobbes or Machiavelli, one moves away from a form of theological anthropology towards a form of pagan mythology. Hobbes wrote *Leviathan* in the seventeenth century following the English Civil War. This founding text of modern political theory posited that the natural state of humans without government is utter conflict, the 'war of all against all', and that individuals must enter into a social contract, mutually agreeing with one another to have power exerted over them by authorized authority so that they can each have their individual rights protected.[16] John Milbank has called the Hobbesian tradition a heretical political theology, while he identifies the political theology of Machiavelli as pagan.[17] In Machiavelli's *The Prince* (1513), modern political theory was given an even more radical option than social contract: instead of a 'natural state' of war which should be controlled and kept in check by authorized authorities, Machiavelli suggested that an on-going state of perpetual war was the surest way for rulers to maintain power and order. In Machiavelli, the order of political theory was reversed; no longer do visions of creation (and fall) or the good form politics, but politics is given free rein to determine what is prudent for the self-interest of sovereign and state.

Moltmann referred to Carl Schmitt's use of Hobbes as the 'Paganization of Leviathan', in particular with regard to Schmitt's resistance towards the differentiation of spiritual and political powers. Moltmann cited Erik Peterson, who claimed in reference to this tendency in Schmitt, 'Whoever renounces the "Jewish-Christian" division of political unity, ceases to be a Christian and has chosen paganism'.[18] For Michael Kirwan, the problem is one of legitimizing versus challenging regimes. In Hobbes and Schmitt, Leviathan claims 'religious legitimacy for itself', which makes this ideology a form of 'political mythology' in contrast to 'political theology', which Kirwan argues must always invoke religious authority 'as a challenge to a regime or authority'.[19]

Thus, while the categories of optimism versus pessimism are oversimplified, if not entirely mistaken as labels for the political theologies of St Augustine and St Thomas, it is nonetheless important to note how the trajectories of Augustinian and Thomistic political thought do have an essential difference which grows out of how the two saints differed on the relationship between creation, politics and the fall. Furthermore, while it is important to see how the Augustinian trajectory has in a certain sense been taken up in the political theory of modern liberalism (which we will discuss in Chapter 6) one should take care not to conflate Hobbesianism with Augustinianism.

THEOLOGICAL AND ECCLESIAL TRADITIONS

Another way to demarcate political theologies is in relation to the theological and ecclesial traditions from which they arise. Though there is no single political theology which represents each distinct form of Christianity, it is nevertheless possible to discern particular emphases and trajectories in political thought which are associated with various theological and ecclesial traditions. We will consider some of the distinguishing characteristics of Roman Catholic, Lutheran, Reformed, Anglican, Anabaptist and Eastern Orthodox traditions.

Roman Catholic political theology is often most associated with themes and trajectories from various forms of Thomism. These include especially the themes of the common good and natural law. While some Roman Catholic theologians embrace the label 'political theology', in terms of the official teachings of the magisterium the chosen label is Catholic Social Teaching. For the past 300 years there has been a growing body of papal encyclicals, bishops' conference statements and council documents which make up official Catholic Social Teaching. Unofficial Catholic Social Teaching consists of the academic work of theologians and the activist work of social movements, and often influences official teaching. The central norms of Catholic Social Teaching include human dignity, solidarity, the common good, peace and justice. In the modern era, Catholic Social Teaching has been critical of both Marxism and certain forms of capitalism and encyclicals have addressed issues such as labour, war, individualism, development, liberation, consumerism, abortion and euthanasia.[20]

Martin Luther's political theology has been identified as a root of extremely divergent political movements. On the one hand, Luther's programme of reformation, which questioned both ecclesial and secular authorities and asserted the equality of all people before God without human intermediaries, can be identified as one source of the impulses which led to modern democracy and to modern liberalism's focus on the individual. On the other hand, his doctrine of the two kingdoms, which we will discuss in Chapter 3, has been associated with the sorts of political quietism and conservatism which permitted the rise of the Third Reich in Germany.[21] However, many Lutherans would contest the idea that political passivity is inherent in Lutheran theology.[22] Furthermore, the legacy of Lutheran political theology is not determined by Luther alone. Arguably one of the most important figures in twentieth-century political theology was the German Lutheran Dietrich Bonhoeffer. We will also return to Bonhoeffer in Chapter 3.

Reformed political theology, that is the political theology of churches and traditions arising from Calvin's and Zwingli's wing

of the Reformation, differs from both Catholic and Lutheran traditions in important ways, as it tends to be at once more sceptical about sin and human nature than Catholic thought yet more
optimistic about transformation and social activism than Lutheran
thought. John Calvin famously instituted an experimental settlement between church and government in Geneva, which has often
been called a theocracy but is perhaps more accurately called a
commonwealth. Calvin saw the civil government and the church
as having distinct purposes, but interrelated and overlapping roles.
There was no clear 'two kingdoms' separation between the 'secular' and 'sacred' spheres; there was one sphere with church and
governmental authorities serving as equal partners but exercising different powers. This arrangement included a Consistory (an
ecclesiastical court), a Company of Pastors (the Synod) and the
Deaconate as a social welfare system. On the one hand, Reformed
political theology has a strong or optimistic view of human government in that it is seen as a channel and subject of the sovereignty
of God and those who hold government offices are seen as min-
isters of God. Thus, like Thomistic political theology, Reformed
political theology holds that government has positive, constructive
functions, not only negative (restraining and punishing) functions.
However, Reformed theology has a much more pessimistic anthropology, seeing humans as hopelessly bound by sin and unable to
find God or discern God's will apart from divine intervention and
revelation. Perhaps this tension is one of the sources of the somewhat paradoxical history of Reformed political theology, which has
been both the most emphatic about the Christian's duty of obedience to government as appointed by God, and also has given rise to
some of the most clear articulations of when government should be
resisted. Some would credit Reformed political theology with both
the rise of apartheid in South Africa as well as one of the earliest
and clearest official ecclesial rejections of it – the World Alliance of
Reformed churches declared apartheid a heresy in 1982.

Because of the historical complexities of the English Reformation,
Anglican political theology, like Anglican theology and worship,
can be either very Catholic or more Reformed; some Anglicans
consider themselves Catholics while others understand their faith
to be Protestant. Some more Catholic Anglicans have remained in
close dialogue with and response to the tradition of Catholic Social
Teaching, while more Protestant Anglicans have had much more

Reformed sensibilities. There is no official body of Anglican Social Teaching, nor is there a towering Anglican figure analogous to Aquinas, Luther or Calvin. However, the social and political witness of the church has been a central aspect of Anglican theology and practice, especially since the nineteenth century. Important figures and movements include William Wilberforce and abolition, F. D. Maurice and Christian Socialism, William Temple on social welfare, opposition to apartheid by Michael Ramsey and Desmond Tutu, and the 'Faith in the City' report which was written under the archbishopric of Robert Runcie.

The Anabaptist tradition has distinctive views which emphasize the separation of church and state as well as complete renunciation of violence by Christians. Anabaptism began during the Reformation when some German, Swiss and Dutch reformers broke away from Luther and Zwingli primarily over the practice of baptism. In the sixteenth century, Anabaptist convictions about baptism and government were inextricably linked. For them, infant baptism was the practice of the established church which was wielding powers from which Christians should be separate, thus separation of church and state and the rejection of infant baptism went hand in hand. Also central to the Anabaptist tradition is absolute pacifism. The duties of enemy love, reconciliation and returning good for evil along with the witness of Jesus' life, teachings and death are seen as excluding the possibility of justified violence for Christians. These convictions have been lived differently in different communities arising from this tradition. For the Amish and Old Order Mennonites, Anabaptist convictions must be lived out in a community which is entirely distinct from the rest of society and practises non-involvement in all governmental affairs. For most other Mennonites and various Brethren churches, the Anabaptist witness is meant to be lived out within society, seeking its transformation without wielding governmental power or using violence. For example, the Mennonite Central Committee operates relief, development, education, reconciliation and peacemaking projects around the globe.

In the following chapters, the least represented theological tradition is the Eastern Orthodox. Eastern Orthodox political theology is such a distinct tradition from the Western forms represented here as to be beyond the scope of this brief introduction. In the West, Eastern political theology has often been caricatured as upholding the absolute unity of church and state, as being overly concerned with order and stability and as being too 'other worldly' or ascetic to positively contribute to the social order. However, contemporary theologians of both the East and the West have revealed very different resources and realities within the political theology of the Orthodox tradition which calls these stereotypes into question, offering resources for material, structural and realist contributions to politics and examples of Eastern Orthodox Christians who have stood against repressive power and in solidarity with the poor and oppressed.[23]

THE FIRST GENERATION: POLITICAL, LIBERATION AND PUBLIC THEOLOGIES

Both historical and contemporary variations of political theology can be classified based on optimism versus pessimism regarding the human condition, or based on the particularities of different theological traditions. Other ways of categorizing political theologies do so with reference to perspectives within the discipline since it was recognized as such in the twentieth century. Daniel M. Bell and Gaspar Martinez have each described the discipline as having three distinct strands: Political Theology, Liberation Theology and Public Theology.[24]

Political Theology

Political Theology 'proper'[25] is the movement which emerged in Germany in the 1960s, particularly in the work of Johann Baptist Metz, Jürgen Moltmann and Dorothee Sölle.[26] These authors sought to call into question the privatization of bourgeois Christianity and re-empower the church to become 'the herald of an eschatological future that always calls into question the status quo, destabilizing the present in the name of a peace, justice, and freedom to come'.[27] The status quo of European Christianity (and in particular for these theologians, German Christianity) was in need of critique for several reasons. First, there was the continuing struggle of Germans to understand how the Nazi regime had come to power, enacted fascist totalitarianism and perpetrated the Holocaust – all in a 'Christian' nation. Where was the church? What had become of German Christianity that it had so little voice or will in opposition to the Nazi horrors? These questions were in no way impersonal for the Political Theologians; Sölle's adolescence had been subsumed in the realities of living in Nazi Germany, while Metz and Moltmann had both been drafted into the German military at a young age.

Second, there were philosophical and theological inheritances from the previous generation which were coming to be seen as problematic in ways which unfit Christianity for the task of being a social presence, particularly the transcendentalism of Martin Heidegger and its outworking in the Catholic theology of Karl Rahner and the Protestant theology of Rudolf Bultmann. The Political Theologians, while not rejecting these approaches altogether, critiqued the dangers of transcendental theology removing faith from its historical and social moorings and locating it instead in the private, existential realities of the individual.

Third, these thinkers were increasingly informed by the rising school of thought now called 'critical theory'. While 'critical theory' is now an umbrella term which covers a considerable variety of philosophical and sociological scholarship,[28] it also refers specifically to a movement which began in early-twentieth-century Germany in which the insights of Karl Marx were wed with other recent and contemporary thinkers, especially Carl Jung and Sigmund Freud in psychology, Max Weber in sociology and Georg Wilhelm Friedrich Hegel in philosophy. 'The Frankfurt School' is normally identified as the origin and locus of this movement. Its central thinkers included Theodore Adorno and Max Horkheimer; more loosely related but equally influential critical theorists for the Political Theologians were Walter Benjamin and Ernst Bloch. These theorists sought to critically describe and analyse current realities, especially as critiques of inequality and injustice, while also making normative, practical claims. Critical theory provided the Political Theologians with ways to interrogate the social shortcomings of contemporary theology through questions such as how a particular theology supports the status quo, whose interests are served by it, how it relates theory to practice and whether it promotes or hinders justice.

Metz's work has focused in particular on the significance of theodicy (the problem of how evil can exist if God is good and all-powerful), particularly in relation to Auschwitz, and of apocalyptic eschatology for political theology.[29] Moltmann has also focused on eschatology, sharing with Metz the influence of eschatological concepts in contemporary German philosophy such as 'anticipation', but for Moltmann the key Christian eschatological theme is hope, and he identified a dialectic of cross and resurrection in relation to the coming kingdom of God which formed the structure of his political theology.[30] Sölle's work was profoundly shaped by reflection upon the Holocaust, though her reflections led her to more radical conclusions than Metz or Moltmann, including rejection of the idea of divine omnipotence. She was a political activist, mystic and feminist with deep concern for issues of global justice; she sought to develop a 'first world' Liberation Theology.[31]

Perhaps because the life and work of Sölle is less well known than the works of Metz and Moltmann, Political Theology has been criticized as lacking true 'political' and 'liberative' force, being a movement of isolated individual scholars working in academic settings without grassroots activist involvement. However, others also note that the liberative out-workings of the movement are clear in the intimate relationship between Political Theology and the beginnings of (at least some) Liberation Theology.

Liberation Theology

The status of Liberation Theology in relation to Political Theology (and political theology more generally) is not straightforward or uncontested. For example, while *The Blackwell Companion to Political Theology* includes chapters on Liberation Theologies and theologians, Kirwan's introduction to political theology distinguishes between 'European political theology' and 'Latin American Liberation Theology', and declines to include the latter in his volume.[32] Kirwan's exclusion of these perspectives was perhaps primarily due to space, scope and specialization (just as I have neglected perspectives from Orthodox Christianity and the global east). However, it also has to do with the assumption many share that Political Theology was done by European academics in their libraries and studies, while Liberation Theology rose up from the grassroots of Latin America and took to the streets in political activism. Kirwan's anecdote further illustrates this distinction:

'A mischievous academic colleague of mine once set the following exam question: "Liberation Theology gave a voice to the oppressed; European Political Theology gave a voice to disaffected academic theologians. Discuss." '[33]

While the Political Theology of 1960s Germany was fairly straightforwardly a movement within academic theology, albeit with clear implications for churches and political activism, Liberation Theology was from its inception less isolated to the academy; it was a movement within three contexts or levels: the writing of academic texts, the meetings and actions of the bishops and grassroots communities and activism. The most widely known and discussed Liberation Theology is that of the theologians who wrote the books which continue to define the rise and content of the movement. In the 1950s, several Latin American Catholic priests who went to Europe for theological training became influenced by the new openness of Catholic theology in Europe exemplified in *la nouvelle theologie*[34] as well as the emerging dialogue between theologians and critical theorists. Alongside the standard theological texts, these priests studied Marx and Freud. In the 1960s, they began the work of relating their European theological education to their Latin American context. On the one hand, they had witnessed the new openness of Catholic theologians and the magisterium to embracing the strengths of modernity and becoming more serious about addressing its negative social consequences – an openness signalled especially by the Second Vatican Council (1962–65). On the other hand, while Europe made huge gains in wealth and comfort during the 1960s, most of Latin America had become poorer and had witnessed increasing political upheaval and violence. Their contexts of political and economic oppression and volatility made the focus of Vatican II on what to embrace and reject from the Enlightenment seem a distant and peculiarly European project. Their own project would need to relate *la nouvelle theologie* and Vatican II to the realities of the dehumanization of their people through economic exploitation and political repression. One of the sources which significantly formed their approach was economic dependency theory.[35]

This project of the Latin American priest-theologians became the texts of early Latin American Liberation Theology. They were written by Juan Luis Segundo in Uruguay; Leonardo Boff in Brazil; and Gustavo Gutiérrez in Peru. The most well-known text from this movement is Gutiérrez's *A Theology of Liberation*, which was first released in Spanish in 1971, and which argues the twin theses of God's universal and gratuitous love, and God's preferential solidarity with the poor.[36] Both the texts and the lives of the central Liberation Theologians show that they were in no way pure academics isolated from the other levels of the Liberation Theology movement.

The second level of the movement was the official ecclesial level: the work and conferences of the Catholic bishops of Latin America. In 1968, the bishops of Latin America met in Medellín, Colombia to develop pastoral strategy for implementing Vatican II in their context, and issued a document which was deeply influenced by emerging Liberation Theology. From 1968 the Liberation Theologians, especially Gutiérrez, were able to formalize and present their project, and their articulation of theology-as-liberation became central to the bishops' next meeting in Puebla, Mexico in 1979. At Puebla, tensions between Latin American bishops with differing views on liberation, as well as tensions between Rome and Latin America became manifestly apparent. Pope John Paul II was suspicious of Liberation Theology, particularly of the influence of Marxism on Liberation Theologians, and would later oppose them with a severity which has been widely criticized.[37]

The third context of Liberation Theology was at the grassroots level. Priests and members of religious orders were moving into poverty-stricken areas out of a conviction that they should live in solidarity with the poorest and most marginalized members of their societies. Clergy and lay people alike were organizing opposition to their corrupt and oppressive governments. And small groups of Christians were meeting together to study scripture from perspectives of poverty and marginalization. One of the most widely recognized manifestations of grassroots Liberation Theology has been the Basic Christian Communities or base ecclesial communities, which have been most prominent in Brazil. In some places these communities have existed in harmony with the magisterium, and in other places they have experienced serious tensions with church leaders. A central feature in these communities and in Liberation Theology in general, is the study of scripture from within the shared experiences of those who are oppressed and marginalized. From its earliest days, Liberation Theology was intended to be lived out in a virtuous circle of experience, biblical study, praxis (both liturgical and societal) and reflection.[38]

Meanwhile, other forms of Liberation Theology were taking shape both independently of and in response to Latin American Liberation Theology. In North America in particular, Black Theology and Feminist Theology emerged as movements sharing much in common with but not entirely dependent upon Latin American Liberation Theology.

Like the Latin American Liberation Theologians, Black Theologians saw a need to begin political theology not from the Enlightenment-related concerns of European Political Theologies, but from their own experience of the oppression of black people, especially in the American institutions of slavery and segregation. Where Political Theology called into question the privatized bourgeois Christianity of Western Europe, Black Theology called into question the white 'Christianity' of America, which it identified as rife with white supremacy and the failure to identify with the person of Jesus Christ. Black Theologians took up the 'preferential option for the poor' of Liberation Theology, and identified 'the poor' with 'blackness'. As in Liberation Theology, praxis was central; Black Theology was a call to direct action in protest and solidarity, as well as a call for a celebration of black culture. In its beginnings, Black Theology was caught between the Civil Rights Movement on the one hand and the Black Power Movement on the other, thus understandings of praxis included a spectrum ranging from commitment to non-violence to calls for racial revolution. We will return to this tension between Black Power and Civil Rights in our look at the work of Martin Luther King Jr in Chapter 7. The original and still most prolific Black Theologian is James Cone, who actually began publishing his theology of black liberation shortly before Gutiérrez published *A Theology of Liberation*. In *Black Theology, Black Power* (1969), Cone described liberation as central to Christianity and 'blackness' as 'the primary mode of God's presence'. He argued that 'Black Power, then, is God's new way of acting in America'.[39] Soon after, J. Deotis Roberts took a slightly different approach, insisting in *A Black Political Theology* that reconciliation is central but must be accompanied by liberation.[40]

While Black Theology arose first in North America because of the unique experience of African Americans, Feminist Theology arose there first largely because women became established in universities and seminaries earlier than in European faculties which were often connected to or controlled by established churches where women were not yet ordained or employed as theologians. Feminist Theology in North America drew inspiration from several sources. Theologically, the Latin American Liberation Theologians were a central influence for some. Politically, it drew on nineteenth-century feminist and suffrage movements as well as contemporary civil rights and anti-war movements. Philosophically, some Feminist Theologians drew on the texts of European feminist theory, such as those of Simone de Beauvoir. Feminist Theology called attention to the androcentricity, or male-centredness, of Christian theology, both in understandings of God and of humans. It also opened the door to the retelling of stories of women in scripture and in church history. Particularly important for political theology, feminists insisted that 'the personal is political', rejecting the modern, liberal division between public and private spheres of life.

In the global South, Feminist Theology was not only responding to sexism in general, but the political legacies of colonialism, post-war struggles for independence and globalization. Feminist Theologians in the South examined not only their political and ecclesial structures, but also their traditional cultures. Their work served not only to unmask the sexism of traditional cultures, but to mine them for constructive resources for resistance to the types of sexism and oppression which accompanied the neo-colonial condition.[41]

Public Theology

Public Theology is yet another North American strand which followed these German and Latin American antecedents. The Public Theologians sought to find 'public' language and action through which to build societal consensus on moral issues. If the enemy of Political Theology was impotent, bourgeois Christianity and the enemies of Liberation Theology were poverty and oppression, the enemies of Public Theology were sectarian Christianity and the loss of societal moral consensus. Catholic Public Theologians such as David Tracy[42] and Richard John Neuhaus[43] took up the work of John Courtney Murray,[44] while Protestant Public Theologians such as Max Stackhouse[45] and Ronald Theimann[46] sought to build on the work of Reinhold Niebuhr. Instilled with Courtney Murray's understanding of the differing roles of state and civil society, and with Niebuhr's emphasis on sin and its amplification in politics, Public Theologians sought especially to communicate theology within and invigorate the activities of civil society. Particularly noteworthy here for its overlap between Feminist (Liberation) Theology and Public Theology is the work of two Catholic theologians, Rosemary Radford Ruether and Elisabeth Schüssler Fiorenza. We will explore specific examples of the work of Reinhold Niebuhr in Chapter 4 and of Rosemary Radford Ruether in Chapter 7.

Stackhouse has described the difference between Public Theology and Political Theology as having primarily to do with the state/civil society distinction. He suggests that Political Theology 'tends to see politics, focused on a centralized government, as the comprehending institution of society and the primary manifestation and guarantor of public justice'.[47] By contrast, according to Stackhouse, Public Theology understands that 'political parties, regimes and policies come and go; they are always necessary, but they are also the by-product of those religious, cultural, familial, economic and social traditions that are prior to government, and every government is, sooner or later, accountable to them'.[48] Thus, instead of focusing on the centralized state as the primary agent of the transformation of societies, Public Theologians seek to enable Christian 'principles and purposes' to 'work their way through the convictions of the people and the policies of the multiple institutions of civil society where the people live and work and play, that make up the primary public realm'.[49]

These three movements, Political, Liberation and Public Theologies, marked the beginnings of political theology as a distinct discipline within academic theology as well as a reinvigoration in the West of theologically formed political criticism and activism. Martinez has summarized his comparison of the three movements by distinguishing between their *loci theologici* – the theological locus or central site of each movement or school of thought:

> For political theology, the historical defeats and catastrophes, such as Auschwitz, and the need to rescue them constitute that *locus*. For liberation theology, the *locus* must be found in the poor, in the nonpersons, and in their liberation struggle, mainly in Latin America, but also elsewhere. Finally, public theology finds its *locus* in a situation, especially but not only in the United

States, of radical plurality and ambiguity, of radical crisis of modern reason and of the modern self in which the truth and the claims of the 'others' must be heard and theologically assumed.[50]

While many of the authors representing the first generation of Political Theology, Liberation Theology and Public Theology are still actively engaged in these projects, it is also the case that a second generation has now clearly emerged with a different *locus*. Daniel Bell has argued for the importance of this 'emergent tradition' (what I am calling the second generation and what Arne Rasmussen has called 'Theological Politics'),[51] asserting that the three streams of first generation political theology shared in common a 'standard reading of the state and civil society, whereby those institutions are heralded as agents of freedom while the church is shorn of a concrete political presence in favor of an apolitical or at most an abstractly and generally political presence as a custodian of values'.[52] In other words, these authors shared the common goal of calling Christians to understand their Christianity as political and public instead of purely 'spiritual' and 'private', but this was primarily understood within a standard account of the roles of the modern state and of civil society, resulting in goals which involved reform or reinvigoration of these institutions. We turn now to the second generation of political theologians whose goals have more to do instead with the life, worship and witness of the church.

THE SECOND GENERATION: POSTLIBERALISM, RADICAL ORTHODOXY AND 'CONTEXTUAL' THEOLOGIES

While first generation political theology grew out of Christian convictions, it tended to aspire to movement from the particularly Christian towards the shared or universal – from what is peculiar to Christians towards what is 'public' and commonly held. By contrast, Bell suggests that the 'emergent tradition' of political theology does not view statecraft as the primary or ultimate horizon and resists 'the eclipse of the proper public, political character of the church' itself.[53] The shift from state or society to church as central political body has also opened space for more work on the political nature of specific Christian doctrines and practices, such as William Cavanaugh's work on the Eucharist.[54]

While the first generation of political theologians was grappling with European secularism as well as the collapse of the secularization thesis, the second generation has criticized the concept of 'the secular' itself. Is there such a thing as a realm of thought or practice – are there ways of thinking and being – which are entirely devoid of the theological or the metaphysical? Can such a realm be objective, neutral and peaceful as advocates of secularization would suggest? James Smith has said of the schools which I have identified as the first generation of political theology that they sought *correlation* between revelation and the secular, while the schools I am calling second generation 'share in common an assertion regarding the *antithesis* between Christian revelation and the direction of given cultural forms . . . as well as a refusal to concede the criteria for responsible public discourse to the supposed neutrality of the secular'.[55]

The second generation of political theologians also tends to have a different view of modernity. While the first generation can be broadly considered critical friends of modernity, in the second generation we find many more outright critics of modernity. Where the first generation was concerned for the church to find her political voice in relation to and in the midst of modernity, second generation political theologians are more likely to seek to overcome the obstacles and limitations of modernity, usually through the retrieval of resources from various premodern periods.

I suggest that within this second generation we should note three movements or streams within late-twentieth- and early-twenty-first-century theology which have contributed to these shifts in political theology. Each one of these has both inherited much from and substantively overturned one of the previous streams of political theology. While the first generation of political theologians were keen to differentiate their programmes from traditional, systematic or doctrinal theology, the second generation has begun the task of reintegrating political theology within the broader theological enterprise. I suspect that very few of the central figures in these three movements, if asked to what discipline their work belongs, would primarily associate themselves with political theology, though all have made substantial contributions to the discipline.

Postliberalism

Postliberal Theology, mainly associated with American theologians, has called into question the ways in which Public Theology sought to take Christianity 'public' instead of calling into question modernity's public/private dualism. Postliberal political theologians work to show the public and political nature of the church's faith, life and worship. The most formative theological influences for Postliberal political theology have included Augustine, Aquinas and Karl Barth. Stanley Hauerwas, perhaps the most well-known figure in this stream, exemplifies the Barthian and Thomistic influence which has been formative especially of the 'Yale School' of thought,[56] with the addition of the Anabaptist influence which came to him particularly through the life and work of John Howard Yoder. Along with Americans Yoder and Hauerwas, British theologian Oliver O'Donovan is another prominent Postliberal political theologian, though his work is more influenced by Augustine and the Reformed tradition than Thomas or Anabaptism. In the spirit of both Barth and Anabaptism, the Postliberal political theologians tend to do more explicitly biblical work than the other two streams.

Radical Orthodoxy

Radical Orthodoxy, a primarily Anglican and Catholic theological stream, follows Political Theology in its engagement with Continental philosophy but renounces its embrace of the modern secular state and what is now interpreted as its alignment of the kingdom of God with progressive politics. The central theological influences for Radical Orthodoxy are Augustine, Aquinas and *la nouvelle theologie*. Texts of Radical Orthodoxy are more likely to plumb the depths of history and philosophy as sources in contrast to the biblical work of Postliberal texts, and where Postliberals draw explicitly on philosophers they are more likely to be Anglo-American than the Continental philosophical interlocutors of Radical Orthodoxy – though common to both schools of thought is the formative influence of Alasdair MacIntyre.[57] Radical Orthodoxy and Postliberalism share a renewed focus on the politics of the church through a retrieval of premodern resources, and they tend to share an appreciation for Aquinas, but Postliberals are more likely to also focus on the character of pre-Constantinian Christianity while Radical Orthodox political theologians tend to be more interested in medieval Christianity. The Postliberal rejection of the sacred/secular distinction has tended to focus on highlighting the political nature of the sacred, while Radical Orthodoxy has introduced a focus on the theological nature of the supposedly secular. Postliberals have generally resisted identification with any particular political or economic theory, while many texts of Radical Orthodoxy explicitly advocate a combination of constitutional monarchy and Christian socialism. They tend to be critical of the Marxist form of socialism embraced by Liberation Theology and draw instead on nineteenth-century forms of Christian socialism. John Milbank, Graham Ward and Catherine Pickstock are considered to be the central authors of Radical Orthodoxy.[58]

Second generation 'contextual' theologies

Closely following the first generation of Latin American, Feminist and Black Liberation Theologies, a large body of what came to be called 'contextual theologies' arose, especially in the 1980s and 1990s. I use the term 'contextual' in quotes here because it was also soon recognized by many that to refer to some theologies as 'contextual' was to imply that other theologies were undertaken without reference to or influence from specific contexts – which, of course, is impossible. So-called contextual theologies are not the ones with contexts; they are the ones which intentionally and explicitly speak from and to a specific context. Some 'contextual' theologies have been intentional extensions of the Latin American Liberation project for different contexts of oppression, thus theologies of liberation have arisen in Africa, Asia, Eastern Europe and the Middle East.[59] Other 'contextual' theologies are not necessarily liberationist, but are efforts to do theology from within specific cultures outside Europe and America. Somewhat difficult to fully identify with either of these categories is Womanist Theology, a theology for and by black women begun by those who did not find their voices spoken or their lives spoken to in either Feminist or Black Theologies.[60]

More recently there are signs of a shift which might be identified as the beginning of the next generation in this trajectory. A specific example is the collection *Queer Theology*, edited by Gerard

Loughlin.[61] This project takes up the liberative impulses and contextual particularity of Liberation Theology but moves beyond its deconstructive impulses. Had the project of Queer Theology been taken up in the first generation of political theologies, it would likely have been accurately described as Liberation Theology meeting queer theory. However, this is not an adequate description of Loughlin's collection of essays; *Queer Theology* does not function primarily to unmask the heterosexist stories, doctrines and practices of Christianity or society, but to reveal the depth and variety of 'queerness' in the Christian tradition. Here 'queer' means both strange, as 'theology runs counter to a world given over to material consumption, that understands itself as "accidental," without any meaning other than that which it gives to itself', and theology has always 'sought to know the unknowable in Christ'. 'Queer' also means something like gay, but different: 'unlike gay, it names more than erotic interests – a sexual orientation – and it names more than marginal, minority interests. It finds itself curiously central to culture at large, disavowed but necessary for a heterosexual normalcy that defines itself in terms of what it rejects'.[62] The collection is an exploration of the 'queerness' of Christian origins, scriptures, orthodoxy and sacraments.

We have now seen that understanding the work of political theologians is not only a matter of understanding the particular arguments they are making but understanding how to situate those arguments within their locations with respect to each of the sets of issues above. A great deal is revealed about a person's political theology by how she characterizes her theological anthropology, by what particular strand of Christian theology she is working within and by how she relates her work to the variations within the first and second generations of political theology as an academic discipline. Once these associations and conversations become clearer, what first appeared to be a perplexing variety of perspectives and projects becomes a dynamic theological dialogue with a history, particular trajectories and varied (sometimes opposing) methods. This clarification has been the task of Part One. In Part Two we will move to an exploration of some of the major questions and issues within political theology. In the conclusion we will reframe these issues as parts of a theological whole, instead of simply allowing them to stand as a list of interesting topics for political theologians to explore.

ISSUES IN POLITICAL THEOLOGY

CHAPTER 3

THE CHURCH AND THE POLITICAL

At the heart of all other issues in political theology is the issue of the relationship between the church and the political. From the earliest centuries when the church struggled under Roman persecution, to the following centuries in which the early theologians struggled to articulate the relationship of the church to the empire which now tolerated her, to the controversies of the medieval period which pitted papal authority against kingly authority, to the radical shifts of the Reformation and the rise of the modern nation-state, to secularization and the separation of church and state: this is the issue which has never fallen out of view of Christian political theology.[1] So long as the kingdom of God exists for us as an already-but-not-yet reality, that is until Jesus returns, the church is perpetually faced with this question: If God is the only true king, if the church is in any sense the body on earth which represents the reign of Christ at the right hand of God the Father, and if human government is in any sense part of God's plan for the ordering of human life, what then is the relationship between church and government?

In the patristic era, this dilemma centred on the relationship between the church and the Roman Empire. Theologians such as St Ambrose and St Augustine looked on the empire warily and believed the church should have the distance and the integrity to call into question the ways of the empire, even in the age of official tolerance of Christianity. Other theologians, like Eusebius and St John Chrysostom, associated the empire more closely with the divine will and the coming kingdom and were grateful for a government which could be the protector and maintainer of the church.

In the medieval era, there were shifting and evolving agreements and tensions between the popes and the monarchs of Europe which culminated in the 'Investiture Controversy' of the eleventh and twelfth centuries. Pope Gregory VII was convinced that his papal power extended to the ability to invest civil rulers with authority, while King Henry IV was convinced that his authority as king extended to the ability to invest bishops with authority in the local church. The controversy led to Gregory twice excommunicating Henry and installing another king to replace him, as well as Henry installing Clement III as pope to replace Gregory. This dispute over whether and in what senses popes or kings had authority over one another continued long after both Gregory and Henry were dead. In the late middle ages, the idea of the king's two bodies arose, theorizing that monarchs in their divine appointments have a natural body which dies and a mystical body which lives on, and these fulfil his two offices. In analogy with Christ, the monarch was thought to have a kingly/human office and nature as well as a divine/priestly office and nature. The king's two bodies, or 'sacral kingship', continued to influence views of monarchs' authority in the churches within their realms well into the modern era.

From the sixteenth century, political theology (along with both political and theological realities) was dramatically transformed. Over a period of just a few centuries, nearly all the most seemingly fixed arrangements of the church and the political would be unmoored and unravelled. After the Reformation, there would no longer be one Christian church in the West. The conversation on the authority of the pope versus the authority of the monarch would splinter into disputes over the relationship of each ruler to the type of religion practised within the realm. And the nature of the realms and rulers was shifting as medieval arrangements faded and the modern nation-state began to come into view. This moved the conversation further, as the authorities in question were no longer the persons of pope and king, but the entities of churches and states. The economies of the newly forming nation-states were also innovations, as feudal configurations were slowly replaced by burgeoning capitalism.

Also during this pivotal time, Europe descended into over a century of intermittent wars which have come to be called the

'Wars of Religion',[2] and which raised for many the idea that nation-states would be less prone to conflict with one another if secularized; that if church authority and state authority were entirely separated from one another, a century of such wars would never be repeated. As secularized states became the norm in the West and the church in many senses became 'de-politicized', various sorts of arrangements of church and state developed. In post-revolution France, there was hope that the secular state would provide freedom *from* religion; the goal was to remove the repressive power of religion from society. In America, there was hope that having no officially established church would provide maximum freedom *for* religion; the goal was toleration of the free exercise of religion which was seen to enhance and vivify society. In England, both the monarchy and the established church remained but the medieval struggles over authority ceased as there was no longer an ecclesial head pitted against the monarch, and the monarch's power was dramatically reduced by the growing role of the parliament.

However, by the 1930s it was becoming clear that the politically secularized West had not become the peaceful and tolerant community of nation-states imagined in the optimisms of early modernity. The entire world had been at war, a generation had been lost and another world war was looming on the horizon. The question of the church and the political had shifted yet again to questions of the moral role of churches within nation-states.

In the remainder of this chapter we will look at one of the most widely criticized yet deeply influential theological articulations of the relationship between church and government: Martin Luther's doctrine of the two kingdoms. It is important to set this doctrine within the context of Luther's life and shifts in his thought. It is also important to understand the doctrine as it continues to have significant influence, despite its rejection by so many theologians. Many critics of the doctrine have suggested that the political marginalization of the church which was the legacy of the two kingdoms is one of the reasons why so many German Christians did not resist Hitler's rise to power or the policies of the Third Reich. We will look briefly at the struggle between church and state in Hitler's Germany and how two of the most influential theologians of the twentieth century, Karl Barth and Dietrich Bonhoeffer, responded in terms of their articulations of church and state.

MARTIN LUTHER (1483–1546)

Luther originally set out to reform the Catholic Church from within. When he nailed his famous *Ninety-five Theses* to the door of the church in Wittenberg in 1517, it was as a Catholic theologian raising questions about some of the practices of his own church. He could not have foreseen that only a few years later he would be excommunicated by the pope and looked upon as the leader of a new church. However, in 1520 with Leo X's papal bull *Exsurge Domine*, the handwriting was on the wall: Luther's reforms were officially rejected and something separate – eventually to be called Protestantism – was taking shape. This raised the crucial issue of his personal status as well as the status of Protestant groups in the eyes of the German princes. Shortly after *Exsurge Domine* was issued, Luther wrote his *Appeal to the Christian Nobility of the German Nation* (1520). In it, his interest in building and maintaining good relations with the princes is clear. This is not to suggest that his motives were entirely pragmatic; the *Appeal* is also a stage in the development of Luther's political theology. Luther had interests in continuing his reformation work, in seeking protection for those putting his reforms into practice and in working out what the relationship between the authority of the church and the authority of secular rulers might be in the absence of the centralization of ecclesial authority in the papacy. In the *Appeal*, Luther suggested that the concept that temporal powers have no authority over spiritual powers was a wall built by 'the Romanists' to protect themselves from challenges to papal authority. Luther was determined to tear down this wall, and the central idea through which he began to work out his theory was the priesthood of all believers. He argued that 'all Christians are truly of the spiritual estate, and there is no difference among them, save of office alone' because 'we are all consecrated as priests by baptism'.[3] Thus, in place of the late medieval understanding of one government with two estates (the temporal and the spiritual), he proposed that within the priesthood of all believers there are none who have exclusive claim to the spiritual estate, and in fact 'temporal power is baptized as we are, and has the same faith and Gospel, we must allow it to be priest and bishop, and account its office an office that is proper and useful to the Christian community'.[4]

   In his efforts to reject the Roman hierarchy and to find favour in its stead with the German princes, Luther's proposal in effect

stripped the church of political power and significance. He concluded that 'a priest should be nothing in Christendom but a
functionary'.[5] Perhaps he did not at first realize the full impact of
so dramatically calling into question ecclesial authority, while giving so much free reign to temporal authority:

> Therefore I say, forasmuch as the temporal power has been
> ordained by God for the punishment of the bad and the
> protection of the good, therefore we must let it do its duty
> throughout the whole Christian body, without respect of
> persons, whether it strikes popes, bishops, priests, monks, nuns,
> or whoever it may be.[6]

It was not long before Luther's views developed further and he
seems to have wanted to redress the radical marginalization of
the church which was the effect of the *Appeal* when he wrote *On
Secular Authority* in 1523.[7] In November of 1522, George Duke of
Saxony issued an edict against Luther's New Testament; it was no
longer to be bought or sold and all existing copies were to be sur-
rendered. What then comes of Luther's eagerness for temporal rulers to punish wayward religious leaders when their sword is turned
on him? In writing *On Secular Authority*, Luther had a slightly
different set of interests: upholding his understanding of government and the sword, based on Romans 13, as well as his challenge
to the papacy, while also protecting himself and the Reformation
in general from secular rulers who would seek its end. His tone has
changed dramatically; no more deference for the princes. '[S]ince I
was not afraid of their idol the pope when he threatened me with
the loss of heaven and my soul', he wrote defiantly, 'I must show the
world that I am not afraid of the pope's lackeys either, who threaten
me [only] with the loss of my life and worldly possessions'.[8]

No longer is the emphasis on the priesthood of all believers and
its equalization of all under the temporal authorities ordained by
God. If a distinction cannot be made which suggests hierarchy
within the body of Christ, a distinction must be made between two
kingdoms instead: the kingdom of God and the kingdom of this
world. Christ rules over the kingdom of God, but he taught that his
kingdom is not of this world. This is a spiritual kingdom of love,
justice and order; it is the ideal of human life apart from sin where
there is no need for law, punishment or any use of violence. As ruler
of this kingdom, Christ is the only authority over all that which is

inward and spiritual. If every human were a perfect Christian, this would be the all-encompassing reality of life. However, humans remain sinful even as redeemed, and thus there must be a kingdom of this world where secular rulers have authority and must wield the sword to maintain the peace. These rulers have authority over outward and bodily matters as they pertain to common life. They have no authority over beliefs or other inward and spiritual matters; Christ is the only authority over the soul. 'Therefore care must be taken to keep these two governments distinct, and both must be allowed to continue [their work], the one to make [people] just, the other to create outward peace and prevent evil-doing. Neither is enough for the world without the other.'[9]

The doctrine of the two kingdoms provided Luther with a new line of attack against the Roman hierarchy – 'They have managed to turn everything upside down: They ought to rule souls with God's Word, inwardly, and instead they rule castles, towns, countries and peoples, outwardly . . .' – as well as a call for restraint to the princes – 'And the secular lords, who should rule countries and peoples outwardly, do not do so either . . . they want to rule spiritually over souls, just as the spiritual authorities want to rule in a worldly manner'.[10]

Although this doctrine of the two kingdoms would later come to be understood as the centre of Luther's political theology, Luther himself was soon to change his view again on temporal authority over spiritual matters. When faced with peasants' revolts, the rise of Anabaptism and radical apocalyptic groups, he would return to his earlier emphasis on the duty of temporal authorities to punish wrongdoing – including heresy – insisting that these groups must be brutally suppressed and punished.

The marks of one Augustinian trajectory of political theology are clear in Luther's doctrine of the two kingdoms, and indeed he likely understood the two kingdoms as a rearticulation of the two cities for his time. However, two key differences between Augustine's two cities and Luther's two kingdoms should be noted. First, the intermingling of the two cities is removed in the stark division between Luther's two kingdoms. While the two cities are two intermingling realities which cannot be neatly separated, apart from their difference in orientation towards God or self, for Luther one of the keys of the doctrine is the strict separation and neat delineation between the two kingdoms. Second, one aspect of the clear delineation between the two kingdoms that, in Luther, the kingdom of God deals with that which is spiritual and inward while the worldly kingdom has authority over that which is bodily and outward. This distinction of inward and outward is foreign to Augustine's two cities. While many mistakenly attribute this inner/outer dualism to Augustine – understandably so, due to the influence of Neo-Platonism on much of his thought – this dualism is not present in Augustine's descriptions of the two cities. Both cities encompass and are related to inward and outward, personal and public, spiritual and corporeal realities. Their distinction is not in the matters of life with which they are concerned, but in the orientation of their concerns in all of life.

KARL BARTH (1886–1968) AND DIETRICH BONHOEFFER (1906–45)

In the face of the rise of National Socialism in Germany and the atrocities of Hitler's regime, we find articulations of the relationship between church and state from two of the foremost German Protestant theologians of the day which sought to reject Luther's two kingdoms. Central to the theologies of Barth and Bonhoeffer and the Confessing Church in which they were leading figures was a reaffirmation of the lordship of Christ over all spheres of human life, including government.

Dietrich Bonhoeffer was a Lutheran pastor and theologian whose career spanned the years of Hitler's rise to power and World War II. He received his theological training in Germany as well as at Union Theological Seminary in New York, where he was deeply influenced by African-American Christianity in Harlem. He returned to Germany just as Hitler was coming to power, and he was critical of Hitler from the beginning, especially his efforts to incorporate the German churches into his regime. Bonhoeffer was executed just before the end of the war for his association with the plot to assassinate Hitler.[11]

Karl Barth was a Swiss Reformed pastor and theologian who was a professor in Germany during Hitler's rise to power. After completing his theological education in Germany and serving as a pastor for ten years in Switzerland, he returned to Germany to teach at Göttingen, Münster and Bonn between 1921 and 1935. He then returned to Switzerland, where he taught and lived the rest of his life and where he wrote the majority of his epic *Church Dogmatics*.[12]

Barth and Bonhoeffer were in close contact with one another in the late 1920s and early 1930s, as Germany attempted to recover from one war and began to mobilize for another. They shared intense mutual concern for the relationship of German Christianity to the changing German state. When Hitler became Reich Chancellor in 1933, this relationship changed dramatically. In July 1933 the Nazis negotiated a concordat with the Vatican which stipulated that the Catholic Centre Party would disband. Hitler severely limited the likelihood and power of German Catholic opposition fairly straight-forwardly in this single act. With the Protestant churches, the process was slightly more protracted. Hitler moved to centralize authority in the Protestant churches under the Reich. Regional churches were required to unify under a single national bishop. Those who were happy to follow Hitler's plan for the churches became known as the *Deutsche Christen*, the German Christians, while those who opposed Nazi control of the churches formed the Pastors' Emergency League. Each of these groups put forward candidates for Reich bishop, and though the Emergency League's candidate was chosen he was so undermined by German Christians' disputes over the elec-tion results that he soon resigned and the pro-Nazi candidate was installed. As part of Hitler's Reich, the unified church was under the authority of the 'Aryan paragraph' or 'Aryan clauses', government regulations excluding Jews and those married to Jews from govern-ment office as well as many other positions in German society, now to include ministry in the church. Those who had been involved in the Emergency League decided it was time to break away from the national church, though they did not consider themselves schismat-ics; rather their title, the Confessing Church, indicated their convic-tion that they were the ones confessing true Christian doctrine in opposition to the German Christians' break with orthodoxy.

In September of 1933, Bonhoeffer wrote to Barth, noting that Barth had published (in a booklet which would be the first of a series under the title *Theological Existence Today*)[13] that an explicit adoption of the Aryan clauses by the German church would mean that the church had ceased to be Christian. The newly united Reich church had officially adopted the clauses under the leadership of the Reich bishop, and Bonhoeffer wanted to know if Barth would follow through with his previously published condemnation. 'We have in the first place drawn up a declaration,' Bonhoeffer wrote, 'in which we wish to inform the church authorities that, with the

Aryan Clauses, the Evangelical Church of the Old Prussian Union has cut itself off from the Church of Christ'.[14] Bonhoeffer was able to guess what Barth's reply might be to the possibility of leaving the state church. 'I know that many people now wait on your judgment,' he wrote. 'I also know that most of them are of the opinion that you will counsel us to wait until we are thrown out.'[15] Barth replied immediately, saying that Bonhoeffer's declaration should be issued, followed by more like it, and that they should then wait either 'until the scandal is done away with – or until the church answers by evicting or muzzling those who protest'. He was not unwilling to consider a break with the Reich church, 'But that can only be a last resort for us,' he wrote.[16]

The declaration referred to in this correspondence became a draft for the call to pastors to join the Emergency League. When the league moved towards the formation of the Confessing Church, Bonhoeffer was asked to write their confession of faith, but this time his draft was rejected, at roughly the same time as he would have received the letter from Barth urging patience in the cause. Exasperated, the following month he left Germany for London, where he became the pastor of two Lutheran churches. When Bonhoeffer wrote to Barth after his arrival in London, Barth replied with a brutally honest letter chastising Bonhoeffer for leaving. 'I just will not allow you to put such a private tragedy on the stage in view of what is at stake for the German church today,' he wrote. '[Y]ou must now leave go of all these intellectual flourishes and special considerations, however interesting they may be, and think of only one thing, that you are a German, that the house of your church is on fire, that you know enough and can say what you know well enough to be able to help and that you must return to your post . . .'[17] Bonhoeffer did not immediately return, and while he was still in London Barth became the main author of the confession which was adopted by the first synod of the Confessing Church at Barmen, May 1934. Though Bonhoeffer was not the author of the Barmen Declaration, he would call the Confessing Church members to it again and again over the remainder of his life.

In August of 1934, Hitler took on unprecedented powers as Germany's Führer. Largely due to his refusal to swear an oath of loyalty to Hitler, Barth left Germany and returned to Switzerland in 1935, where he would teach for nearly 30 years and enjoy a brief retirement until his death in 1968. Bonhoeffer continued to be torn

between leaving Germany in protest and returning to aid in resistance. He returned in 1935 to teach in the Confessing Church seminary. The seminary was closed in 1937 and by 1939 the prospect
of conscription into Hitler's army was looming heavily; Bonhoeffer
departed again to teach in America. Within months he felt he
could not be sheltered from the war at a distance, and returned to
Germany where he avoided conscription through joining an anti-
Nazi conspiracy movement which was operating under the cover of
the *Abwehr*, the military intelligence. Bonhoeffer's precise role in
the *Abwehr* conspiracy to assassinate Hitler is not clear, but for his
association with the conspirators he was imprisoned in 1943 and
executed on 9 April 1945, mere weeks before Hitler's death.

In one sense, Bonhoeffer never entirely broke from a Lutheran
view of church and state. Writing in May of 1933 to call into question Nazi policies towards Jews, Bonhoeffer affirmed a strict division between political and spiritual authorities.

> Without doubt, the Church of the Reformation has no right to
> address the state directly in its specifically political actions. It
> has neither to praise nor to censure the laws of the state, but
> must rather affirm the state to be God's order of preservation in
> a godless world; it has to recognise the state's ordinances, good
> or bad as they appear from a humanitarian point of view, and
> to understand that they are based on the sustaining will of God
> amidst the chaotic godlessness of the world . . . The true church
> of Christ . . . which lives solely from the Gospel and realises the
> character of the state's actions, will never intervene in the state
> in such a way as to criticise its history-making actions, from the
> standpoint of some humanitarian ideal. It recognises the absolute
> necessity of the use of force in this world and also the 'moral'
> injustice of certain concrete acts of the state which are necessarily
> bound up with the use of force. But that does not mean that it
> lets political action slip by disinterestedly; it can and should . . .
> continually ask the state whether its action can be justified as
> legitimate action of the state . . . In so doing it does not encroach
> on the state's sphere of responsibility, but on the contrary fathers
> upon the state itself the whole weight of the responsibility for its
> own particular actions . . . *qua* church it will only ask whether
> the state is bringing about law and order or not.[18]

Thus, in relation to the treatment of Jews by the German state, the division of two spheres of authority prevents the church from rebelling against the state if the motive is that its racial policies are inhumane. However, according to Bonhoeffer, while the church has no right to usurp the authority of the state by calling its particular actions unjust or inhumane, the state likewise has no right to usurp the authority of the church through interfering with its proclamation of the gospel. In this way, the dividing wall of Luther's two kingdoms remains intact.

However, Bonhoeffer did break with some aspects of Luther's thought. First, he went farther than Luther who had said that when the state encroaches on the church's spiritual authority, the appropriate response is simply to disobey in regard to the specific encroachment (e.g. if the prince prohibits the possession of a certain New Testament, the church should not surrender their copies). Bonhoeffer clears the way for more direct action against the state. 'The church must reject this encroachment of the order of the state precisely because of its better knowledge of the state and of the limits of its action. The state which endangers the Christian proclamation negates itself.'[19] The church has three possible courses of action in response to wrong-doing on the part of the state: (1) ask if the state's efforts at law and order are justifiable in terms of keeping law and order, (2) aid the victims of the state if its law and order functions cause harm (3) take direct political action if (and *only if*) the state fails to bring law and order (by either providing too much or too little of either or both) to the extent that the existence of the state and the church is threatened. 'The third possibility is not just to bandage the victims under the wheel but to put a spoke in the wheel.'[20] Thus, in relation to policies towards Jews, Bonhoeffer wrote that the church should be asking questions about whether specific racial policies served the causes of law and order, as well as helping Jews who were hurt by current policies. And they should now stand at the ready, considering whether and when it might be time to take the third possibility, the last resort of direct action which inhibits the state.

Second, and increasingly as the Nazi regime gained more power over the German churches and began to mobilize for war, Bonhoeffer was critical of how Luther's two kingdoms marginalized Christ's reign and way of life, making the church invisible in the world. The following is an excerpt from Bonhoeffer's lectures to students in the Confessing Church seminary.

> [I]n his own way Luther confirms Constantine's covenant with the church. As a result, a minimal ethic prevailed. Luther of course wanted a complete ethic for everyone, not only for the monastic orders. Thus the existence of the Christian became the existence of the citizen. The nature of the church vanished into the invisible realm. But in this way the New Testament message was fundamentally misunderstood, inner-worldliness became a principle. Therefore today we must be concerned with the witness to its application to the outer world. According to the witness of the New Testament, the church is the city on the hill.[21]

In his *Ethics*, a posthumously published collection of manuscripts written between 1940 and 1943, Bonhoeffer emphasized the lordship of Jesus Christ over human government. 'So long as the earth continues, Jesus will always be at the same time Lord of all government and Head of the Church . . .'[22] For Bonhoeffer, the Lordship of Christ over both spheres eliminates the possibility, opened by Luther's two kingdoms, of two different ethical standards. 'From this there follows the denial of the idea of a double church morality, i.e. one morality for the world and another morality for the congregation . . . one for the Christian in the secular sphere and another for the *homo religiosus*.'[23] Bonhoeffer rejected notions that the ethic of Jesus was only for the personal and spiritual sphere while the ethic of the Old Testament could be applied to the political and temporal sphere. 'Both apply to both world and congregation. The assertion that it is not possible to govern with the Sermon on the Mount arises from a misunderstanding of the Sermon on the Mount.'[24] He also rejected the compartmentalization of the individual life into separate spheres. '[I]t is the Christian who is at once labourer, partner in marriage, and subject of government. No division into separate spheres or spaces is permissible here. The whole man stands before the whole earthly and eternal reality, the reality which God has prepared for him in Jesus Christ.'[25]

Barth shared with Bonhoeffer these convictions about the relationship between the lordship of Jesus Christ and the role and authority of the state, and this is reflected in the *Barmen Declaration*.[26] In this declaration, the Confessing Church members proclaimed along with Barth their rejection of several 'false doctrines' regarding church and state, including the following:

> We reject the false doctrine that there could be areas of our life in which we would not belong to Jesus Christ but to other lords . . . that the Church could, and could have permission to, give itself or allow itself to be given special leaders [Führer] vested with ruling authority . . . that beyond its special commission the State should and could become the sole and total order of human life and so fulfil the vocation of the Church as well . . . that beyond its special commission the Church should and could take on the nature, tasks and dignity which belong to the State and thus become itself an organ of the State.[27]

Luther's two kingdoms can be illustrated as two parallel columns:

	Kingdom of God	Worldly Kingdom
a	Christ is king	secular rulers have authority
b	sword and law not needed	must be ruled by sword and law
c	the ideal apart from sin	required because of sin
d	ethic of love	ethic of coercion
e	makes people just	maintains outward peace through restraint and punishment of evil
f	Jesus' teachings apply here: no retaliation, no violence	retaliation and violence required to protect others, maintain peace
g	concerned with inward and spiritual matters	concerned with outward and bodily matters
h	has authority in matters of belief	has authority in matters of common life

Even if he intended to break further from this doctrine, Bonhoeffer's writings on church and state would still best be illustrated by two parallel columns with a strict division between the matters of concern and the extent of authority, but with several important differences (italicized):

	Church	State
a	*Christ is king*	*over all of life*
b	Sword and law not needed	must be ruled by sword and law
c	the ideal apart from sin	required because of sin
d	*one Christian ethic*	*for all of life*
e	makes people just	maintains outward peace through restraint and punishment of evil
f	Jesus' teachings apply here: no retaliation, no violence	retaliation and violence required to protect others, maintain peace
g	concerned with religious matters both inward and outward	concerned with political matters, primarily law and order
h	has authority in matters of belief	has authority in matters of common life

Barth moved slightly further from the two kingdoms doctrine, and though he would not reject the idea of two spheres entirely, he would later write that his own view could be illustrated by the spheres as a series of concentric circles. At the centre is the kingdom of God, the reign of Christ, functioning as the source and goal of all else. The next, inner circle is the church where Christ's reign is recognized and understood. Finally the outer circle is the state, which also grows from and serves the reign of Christ but may do so unwittingly, and cannot understand its purpose as the church does.[28]

It is evident from this exploration of one theory of church and government, as well as some prominent criticisms of it, that understandings of Christ as king are central issues in political theology. As long as we await his return, we will grapple with the relationship of Christ's reign over our lives and our churches to the authority of governmental structures and figures. As complicated a relationship as this is to articulate and live faithfully, it is not the only concern of political theology related to the person of Jesus Christ. In the next chapter, our focus will shift to questions about the significance of the life, teachings and death of Jesus of Nazareth.

CHAPTER 4

THE POLITICS OF JESUS

Throughout most of Christian history, theories of the relationship between the church and the political have generally had little to do with the life and teachings of Jesus Christ. When political theology of the medieval period discussed Christology, it was usually in the form of reflections upon the relationship of the risen and ascended Christ and his kingdom to the temporal politics of human societies. And as we saw in our exploration of Oliver O'Donovan's use of the Bible in Chapter 1, some contemporary political theologians believe this is the appropriate line to take. However, others such as John Howard Yoder and Stanley Hauerwas have contended that the life and teachings of Jesus, as well as his death and resurrection, are more directly politically normative. In other words, they would contend against Luther that the way of life taught and lived by Jesus has relevance to politics, not only to a supposedly non-political, spiritual realm of life. One of the sources of this emphasis in the works of Yoder and Hauerwas is the influence of the Anabaptist tradition on their theology and ethics.[1] I will introduce the sixteenth-century Anabaptists below, and discuss their unique contribution to historical political theology through their insistence upon the normativity of the teachings, life and death of Jesus.

We will then return to the work of John Howard Yoder, especially his book *The Politics of Jesus*. As a twentieth-century Mennonite and scholar of sixteenth-century Anabaptism, Yoder both embraced and challenged aspects of the political theology of their common tradition. While Yoder's work on the political significance of Jesus was in some ways entirely unique and ground-breaking in its day (it was first published in 1972), it is also important to understand *The Politics of Jesus* in relation to a wider conversation in nineteenth- and twentieth-century theology concerning how Jesus understood his own mission and ministry, including its relationship to the political. The 'quest for the historical Jesus' was a movement of scholarly effort to sift through the traditions and scriptures surrounding the life and teachings of Jesus to find the historical reality of what Jesus did, said and believed. The quest in some senses continues, but its philosophy – the idea that it is possible to 'get behind' the sources and traditions in existence to recover the 'actual' teachings and events of Jesus' life – has been seriously challenged. In the nineteenth and early twentieth centuries, the early scholars of the quest generally concluded either that Jesus was apolitical and his life and teachings contained no element of social criticism or political ideology, or that any politically significant elements of his teachings were part of an 'interim ethic', that is, teachings which assumed that people should live in light of the expectation that human history was going to end within a generation.[2] After the mid-twentieth century, this consensus began to unravel, and the sociopolitical dimensions of Jesus' teachings and actions began to come into view.[3] During this period, a debate arose over whether or not Jesus was a Zealot, a Jewish revolutionary advocating the violent overthrow of the Roman occupation.[4] More recently, and partially due to the influence of Yoder's work, more scholars have discussed the politics of Jesus in ways which reject both extremes of apoliticism or interim politics on the one hand and revolutionary politics on the other.[5]

In addition to the question of the nature of the politics of Jesus' life and teachings is the question of whether and/or how the politics of Jesus might be applicable to contemporary political life. Settling questions of Jesus' own political views and actions does not immediately resolve questions of Christian politics today. One of the keys to understanding both the work of Yoder and the disciplines of Christian social ethics and Public Theology in twentieth-century America is knowledge of the work of Reinhold Niebuhr, who insisted that the life and teachings of Jesus cannot be applied to the political. Niebuhr's work has been at the core of the canon of Protestant social ethics in America as well as the Public Theology stream of political theology. It has also enjoyed a small renaissance recently due in part to President Barak Obama's references to

Niebuhr as a formative political influence. It was partially against the pervasive influence of Niebuhr's views on Jesus and politics which Yoder argued in *The Politics of Jesus*. This chapter will close with a look at Niebuhr's views on the politics of Jesus as exemplified in some of his short essays.

ANABAPTISM

In most standard courses and textbooks on the Reformation, students are taught that there were three wings of the Reformation: Magisterial Reformation, Counter Reformation and Radical Reformation (when divided this way, the English Reformation falls within the category of Magisterial). The Magisterial Reformation refers to the movements led by Luther, Calvin and Zwingli and is called 'magisterial' in reference to the views of and relationships with civil authorities held by these reformers. The Counter Reformation refers to the changes within the Catholic Church as opposed to those reformers who became Protestants. The Radical Reformation refers to those who split not only from the Catholic Church but also from the reformation movements of Luther, Calvin and Zwingli, primarily over the issues of baptism and the relationship between the church and civil authorities. However, each of these labels is somewhat contentious. Many Protestants would question why their wing of the Reformation is labelled with reference to one limited aspect of their views, and seems to serve only to define them in opposition to the Radical Reformation. Many Catholics prefer 'Catholic Reformation' to 'Counter Reformation', as the latter seems to privilege the Protestants and view the changes within the Catholic Church as only being afterthoughts to the Protestant Reformation. And many Anabaptists question the label 'radical' as it is often explicitly used to describe this wing as those who took reformation too far; it implies that the reforms of Luther, Calvin and Zwingli were reasonable, respectable Reformation as opposed to other radical, fringe types. The label 'Radical Reformation' is also often used to encompass such a wide range of people and beliefs – many of which are entirely incompatible with one another – that it seems unhelpful as a category except as a way to group together (and often to dismiss) everyone other than those who remained Catholic and those who followed Luther,

Calvin or Zwingli. In relation to politics, the 'Radical Reformation' label is given to groups who were steadfastly pacifist and believed Christians must have no involvement in government as well as to groups who attempted the violent establishment of apocalyptic theocracies.

For historians, this has caused lengthy and lingering debates about who the Anabaptists truly were: were they all those who 're-baptized', regardless of whether they held any other doctrinal or ethical concerns in common? Or is there a true and normative Anabaptism? This is an important discussion for historians of the Reformation,[6] but one with which we do not need to trouble ourselves further here, for one reason: we can say that there is a set of characteristics common to 'true' Anabaptism not in the sense that it describes which of the sixteenth-century groups were truly Anabaptist, but because it describes the type of Anabaptism which has had the clearest lasting legacy and in many ways continues in Anabaptist churches today. Violent, apocalyptic and theocratic movements have a way of dying out within a generation!

With that important qualification in mind, we can identify the Anabaptists as those groups of Reformation Christians, arising in at least three distinct traditions among the Swiss, Germans and Dutch, who parted company with the Magisterial Reformation. They were severely persecuted by Catholics and Protestants alike; martyrdom was a distinct possibility which all Anabaptists had to be willing to face. Their leaders were routinely executed and their members were repressed, pursued, imprisoned and killed across Europe. These distinctive characteristics differentiate them from other reformers: they refused to practise infant baptism, they were committed to the separation of the church from civil powers, they were pacifists in all areas of life, their communities were shaped by the discipline of 'the ban' (the Anabaptist version of excommunication), they were biblicist and primitivist (they believed that the Bible and the earliest Christians were their authority and example, not the teachings, traditions or institutions which had developed since), and they believed that the teachings of Jesus were equally normative for all Christians (in other words, there is not one expectation for clergy or those in religious orders and another for everyone else; all Jesus' teachings are the standard for all Christians).

We took a brief look at some of these distinctive characteristics in Chapter 2, and here we will focus a bit more on the political implications of the normativity of Jesus by looking at a key Anabaptist document, the Schleitheim Confession. The document arose from a gathering in Schleitheim in 1527, two years after the Swiss Anabaptists had formally parted ways with the Magisterial Reformation. It was likely written by Michael Sattler (c. 1490–1527) and intended to describe 'true' Anabaptism in contrast to the Magisterial Reformation, to Catholic and Protestant misinterpretations of Anabaptism and to other versions of Anabaptism. A few months after the Schleitheim gathering Sattler was martyred, suffering a brutal execution which was characteristic of those reserved for 'heretics': his tongue was torn out, he was tortured with hot irons and then burnt to death.

The Schleitheim document included the 'Seven Articles', matters of doctrine and practice which the Swiss Anabaptists considered most distinctive, characteristic and important: adult baptism, the breaking of bread, the ban, separation from the world, shepherds of the church, refusal of the sword and not swearing oaths. Often interpreted as utopian apoliticism, these Anabaptist distinctives are actually all connected by a political thread: their understanding that Jesus Christ demonstrated and calls all his followers to a way of living together which is entirely different from the standard practices of human politics. The standard practices include violence, allegiance to authorities other than God, lack of reconciliation and dominating uses of authority. Together, the articles formed a charter of a counter-polity, a political body marked by the refusal of standard political options in favour of a new option called into being by Jesus Christ. Every individual article appeals to a teaching or command of Christ or to what it means to be the body of Christ.

The lengthiest article is on the sword. In the Reformation era, 'the sword' was shorthand not only for the use of violent force, but for the exercise of civil authority which is marked by the duty and ability to punish wrongdoing. Thus the article 'concerning the sword' contains three sections: 'whether a Christian may or should use the sword against the wicked for the protection and defense of the good, or for the sake of love', 'whether a Christian shall pass sentence in disputes and strife about worldly matters', 'whether a Christian should be a magistrate if he is chosen'.[7] Each of these is answered 'no', because within 'the perfection of Christ' warning and commandments, admonition and exclusion are used for keeping order and punishing wrongdoing – not the sword.

Critics of this view are likely to focus on statements such as 'Christ teaches and commands us to learn from Him, for He is meek and lowly of heart and thus we shall find rest for our souls', and 'the rule of government is according to the flesh, that of the Christians is according to the spirit',[8] to demonstrate that Anabaptists were utopian idealists focused on the world to come. There are at least two important reasons why this is not entirely accurate. First, the refusal of violent means and governmental power is not supported only by an ideal of Christ as meek and lowly, but in the concrete example of his life: 'Christ was to be made king, but He fled and did not discern the ordinance of His Father. Thus we should also do as He did and follow after Him.'[9] Second, there is no utopian vision of a polity in which there needn't be mechanisms in place for keeping order and punishing wrongdoing. There are clear instructions about keeping order non-violently through good leadership, confronting wrongdoing directly and admonishing wrongdoers. And when these fail, instead of relying on violence as a last resort, Anabaptists used the ban. Those who had been confronted twice privately and a third time publicly, according to the teaching of Jesus in Matthew 18, and still failed to be persuaded, would be banished from the community. In other words, the Anabaptists believed that 'those who have given themselves over to the Lord, to walk after [Him] in His commandments; those who have been baptized into the one body of Christ, and let themselves be called brothers or sisters' must order their common life together – must have a different politics – than those who have not given themselves over to the lordship of Christ.[10]

For sixteenth-century Anabaptists, this did not mean that there should be no wars or no violent forms of punishment. They basically shared the same standard interpretation of Romans 13 as all other Christians of their era: that God ordained the use of violence by governmental authorities. Where they differed was in their belief that the sword was ordained 'outside the perfection of Christ', and thus should not be wielded by those who sought to follow Christ.

The sword is an ordering of God outside the perfection of Christ. It punishes and kills the wicked, and guards and protects the good. In the law the sword is established over the wicked for punishment and for death, and the secular rulers are established to wield the same. But within the perfection of Christ only the ban is used for the admonition and exclusion of the one who has sinned, without the death of the flesh, simply the warning and the command to sin no more.[11]

This division of inside and outside the perfection of Christ is a dualism built upon a dualism; it is dependent upon an oppositional view of law and gospel, so that government ordained by God which has not yet submitted to the lordship of Christ continues to operate rightfully under the old law but those Christians seeking to submit themselves fully to Christ must live by the gospel of love. In his twentieth-century retrieval and reappropriation of the Anabaptist tradition, Yoder would affirm the political normativity of Christ while rejecting this dualism.

THE POLITICS OF JESUS (1972)

Yoder's *The Politics of Jesus* opens with his observations on the different reasons why Christians have argued that the ethic of Jesus is irrelevant to the social and political order. Some argue that Jesus taught an interim ethic – a way of living which was dependent upon the belief that he would be returning to earth and ending the current age within the lives of the current generation. Some argue that Jesus' ethical guidance may have been practical to employ only in his socio-historical context; Jesus was a rural figure of the Ancient Near East whose teachings cannot be translated into modern life. Others argue that Jesus and those he taught were in a position of social and political powerlessness, and that a different ethic is required where Christians are no longer in such positions. It has also been argued that Jesus' message was essentially spiritual, not social or political, and/or that the point of the Christ-event is related exclusively to the atonement; Jesus came to teach a spiritual way and die for people's sins and had no concern for political matters. Still others are simply so sceptical about what we can know about what the historical Jesus actually said and did, that they conclude we cannot rely on the teachings recorded in the gospels as normative guidance.

Against all these theories, which Yoder names as ways of evading the ethical normativity of Jesus, he argues that 'the ministry and the claims of Jesus are best understood as presenting to hearers and readers not the avoidance of political options, but one particular social-political-ethical option',[12] and that this particular option must have a normative claim on the Christian life. He asks, 'What becomes of the meaning of incarnation if Jesus is not normative man?'[13] Yoder demonstrates the existence and the shape of this particular option through a discussion of several key moments in Jesus' life in the gospel of Luke. From the annunciation (Luke 1), through the proclamation of John the Baptist (Luke 3), Jesus' baptism and the temptations in the desert (Luke 3 and 4), the reading of the Isaiah scroll in Nazareth (Luke 4), the feeding of the multitudes (Luke 9), teachings on the coming kingdom and the cost of discipleship (Luke 12–14), the 'cleansing' of the Temple – which Yoder calls the 'epiphany in the Temple' (Luke 19), and the confrontation with the soldiers in Gethsemane (Luke 22), to the culmination in his crucifixion, Yoder traces a consistent message and way of being.

Jesus is proclaimed and commissioned, and announces himself, to be about the ushering in of a new era, a coming kingdom. He is repeatedly offered ways of being king which he refuses, but this is not because he is refusing to be political, rather he is choosing the radical political option of ruling through suffering service and gathering a community of disciples which is invited to reign with him in suffering service. The closer he moves to Jerusalem, the more the 'cross is beginning to loom not as a ritually prescribed instrument of propitiation but as the political alternative to both insurrection and quietism'.[14] In other words, Jesus was not avoiding the social and political, saying 'I am not that kind of a ruler; I am a spiritual ruler'. He was saying 'I am not the kind of ruler which humans expect; I am not a violent or dominating ruler, but I will also not fail to rule'. Throughout the gospel, this message is almost entirely lost on the disciples. When Jesus dies they are confused by his failure and conclude that he must not be the Messiah after all; the kingdom had not come. Yoder says, 'they were failing to see that the suffering of the Messiah *is* the inauguration of the kingdom . . . The cross is not a detour or a hurdle on the way to the kingdom; it is the kingdom come'.[15]

According to Yoder, Jesus was offered and sometimes genuinely tempted by several political options: violent insurrection against Roman occupation urged by the Zealots, withdrawal from history into the desert existence of the Essenes, realist collaboration with the powers-that-be as practised by the Sadducees and the

Herodians or the quietism of withdrawal into the separatist sub-culture of the Pharisees.[16] At every turn, Jesus rejects these ways. Instead, he proclaims and inaugurates the coming kingdom which is characterized by liberation and non-violence.

Yoder argues that his presentation of the way of Jesus refuses several binary choices generally given by theologians; I will focus on two here.[17] One is that the kingdom being proclaimed by Jesus was understood by him to be an outward, political reality which would be catastrophic (in other words, that Jesus was making a purely apocalyptic proclamation), or that the kingdom as proclaimed by Jesus was an inward reality (that Jesus was making a purely spiritual proclamation). In contrast, Yoder argues that the kingdom proclaimed and inaugurated by Jesus was concrete and social and not dependent upon the imminent end of human history. 'It does not assume that time will end tomorrow; it reveals why it is meaningful that history should go on at all.'[18]

Another often assumed binary is that there are two choices, the political and the sectarian. We must either choose between accepting and engaging in the realities of governing as they exist, which is the relevant and responsible path, or in our refusal to do so we are relegated to apoliticism and withdrawal into an irresponsible, sectarian existence. On this view, refusal to accept the political status quo is seen as motivated by either an other-worldly focus which sees politics as unimportant or a focus on purity which sees politics as too dirty a business for Christian hands. Those who want to follow Jesus' ethical guidance exclusively will be sectarian; those who wish to be relevant and responsible must supplement and correct for the gaps in Jesus' ethic. Yoder insists that Jesus neither presented himself as, nor was he received as, an apolitical figure.

> *Because* Jesus' particular way of rejecting the sword and at the same time condemning those who wielded it *was* politically relevant, both the Sanhedrin and the Procurator had to deny him the right to live, in the name of both of their forms of political responsibility. His alternative was so relevant, so much a threat, that Pilate could afford to free, in exchange for Jesus, the ordinary Guevara-type insurrectionist Barabbas. Jesus' way is not less but more relevant to the question of how society moves than is the struggle for possession of the levers of command; to this Pilate and Caiaphas testify by their judgment on him.[19]

Nor was the gathering of disciples into a community of his own rule an apolitical agenda for Jesus to pursue. Working within the existing social structures as they are is not the only way to be political, or politically relevant. To suggest that countercultural groups are necessarily apolitical 'is to overrate both the power and the manageability of those particular social structures identified as "political"'.[20] Jesus was unwilling to accept such overestimation of politics-as-usual.

> He refused to concede that those in power represent an ideal, a logically proper, or even an empirically acceptable definition of what it means to be political. He did not say (as some sectarian pacifists or some pietists might), 'you can have your politics and I shall do something else more important'; he said, 'your definition of *polis*, of the social, of the wholeness of being human socially is perverted.'[21]

According to Yoder, central to the political nature of Jesus' life and the life into which Jesus calls the church is the way of non-violence. Yoder carefully distinguishes this way from other forms of pacifism. Jesus' non-violent way is not the way of idealism; it is not a liberal optimism in human nature and what we could achieve if we could all just get along. Nor is it a way of pragmatism; it is not a calculation that 'it is wrong to kill but that with proper nonviolent techniques you can obtain without killing everything you really want or have a right to ask for'.[22] The reason Christians are pacifists, on Yoder's view, is that Christians follow Jesus who did not count equality with God as something to be seized upon, rather he renounced lordship and embraced suffering to the point of dying, as is reflected in the early hymnody in Philippians 2. Yoder quotes from the Christ hymn, which goes on to say that 'the judgment of God upon this renunciation and acceptance of defeat is the declaration that this is victory. "Therefore God has greatly exalted him and given him the title, which every creature will have to confess, *the Lord*."'[23] In other words, Jesus' non-violence was his renunciation of 'the claim to govern history', and 'the universal testimony of Scripture is that Christians are those who follow Christ at just this point'.[24] The non-violent way of Jesus is not merely a commandment not to use violence which Christians are obligated to obey; it is a way of viewing human history and politics in the light of the fact that Jesus is risen and exalted and ruling over human history precisely because he refused to exert his rule in expected (violent, dominating) ways – because of the cross.

> Certainly any renunciation of violence is preferable to its acceptance; but what Jesus renounced is not first of all violence, but rather the compulsiveness of purpose that leads the strong to violate the dignity of others. The point is not that one can attain all of one's legitimate ends without using violent means. It is rather our readiness to renounce our legitimate ends whenever they cannot be attained by legitimate means itself constitutes our participation in the triumphant suffering of the Lamb.[25]

Many readers of Yoder have been disturbed by such suggestions. They find it difficult to believe that renouncing control over history and refusing to pursue legitimate ends through violent means could be anything but acquiescence to oppression and injustice. Renouncing the drive to be responsible and effective must mean resigning ourselves to being irresponsible and ineffectual. Yoder disagrees.

> [T]o follow Jesus does not mean renouncing effectiveness. It does not mean sacrificing concern for liberation within the social process in favour of delayed gratification in heaven, or abandoning efficacy in favour of purity. It means that in Jesus we have a clue to which kinds of causation, which kinds of community-building, which kinds of conflict management, go with the grain of the cosmos, of which we know, as Caesar does not, that Jesus is both the Word (the inner logic of things) and the Lord ('sitting at the right hand').[26]

In his overall argument about the politics of Jesus, and particularly in his presentation of the politics of Jesus as non-violent, Yoder had many critical interlocutors in mind. He was rejecting several specific aspects of the tradition of theological liberalism. He was both constructively employing and calling into question the scholarship surrounding 'the quest for the historical Jesus'. He was interacting critically with his own Anabaptist tradition by affirming the normativity of Jesus while rejecting those aspects of the dualistic tendencies of Anabaptism which were prone to sectarianism and perfectionism. And he also very much had in mind to recapture for Christian ethics (especially in American Protestantism) the normativity of Jesus Christ which he believed had been lost largely due to the pervasive influence of the Christian realism of Reinhold Niebuhr. It is to Niebuhr's view of the politics of Jesus that we now turn.

REINHOLD NIEBUHR (1892–1971)

Reinhold Niebuhr was born in America to German immigrants. His ecclesial roots were in the Evangelical Synod of North America ('evangelical' in the Reformation sense of the word), the American version of a German church with both Calvinist and Lutheran influences. He understood himself as an Augustinian. His work is marked by the rejection of the theological liberalism of his early thought in favour of neo-orthodoxy (as in Paul Tillich and Karl Barth), and the rejection of naïve humanistic optimism in favour of the stream of thought he pioneered, 'Christian realism'.[27] Niebuhr's life and work were also deeply shaped by interactions with his brother and fellow theologian, H. Richard Niebuhr.[28] Theologians who identify themselves with Protestant social ethics and Public Theology are very often Niebuhrians, consciously continuing and building upon Reinhold Niebuhr's legacy.

At the core of his project were his theories of individual human nature and of social human nature. Niebuhr believed that the individual is trapped in the tension between human self-transcendence (the ability to perceive and imagine the universal and the eternal) and human finitude (especially limited knowledge, bound by one's own perspective). Out of this tension humans tend to experience anxiety and to act out in sin. Sin arises from resolving the tension; we either err on the side of transcendence and sin through pride, hunger for power and self-deception or we err on the side of finitude and sin through sensuality and the abdication of responsibility.[29] According to Niebuhr this tension, though difficult, is manageable at the level of the individual. However, sins of pride and sensuality grow exponentially in their number and severity as the size of social groups grows; the larger the group of people, the more difficult it is to manage and correct for human sinfulness. The individual is capable of goodness which societies and nations are not.[30]

In order to understand Niebuhr's view of Jesus' relation to politics, one must also understand his views on love and justice. We will consider two pieces from *Love and Justice*,[31] a collection of short essays (mostly articles printed in periodicals such as *The Christian Century*) which spans Niebuhr's career. The collection shows a stable set of concepts surrounding love, justice and the significance of Jesus, while also showing developments in specifics of his thought and how he related these concepts to particular issues, ranging from his scathing critiques of pacifists and advocates of non-involvement in the years leading up to World War II, to his advocacy of a new world organization (eventually to become the United Nations), to his interaction with labour disputes involving Henry Ford, to his attention to the injustices of racism in America and segregation in the American South.

For Niebuhr, all such social, political and economic discussions must be governed by the norm of justice, not love. He consistently spoke of love in terms of the *agape* of the gospels, the love which led Jesus to completely renounce all self-interest and resistance against evil to the point of dying on the cross. On this understanding love is a rigorous ideal of intentions and motives which are always orientated towards the interests of others instead of the self. It is a passive selflessness of attitude.

By contrast, justice is the active enforcement through coercion and the assertion of rights of an approximation of ideal human sociality (which Niebuhr called 'brotherhood') under the limitations of human sinfulness. Where selflessness and self-sacrifice are the formative principles governing love, liberty and equality are the formative principles governing justice. Where the moral path of love is always the clear path of selflessness, the path of justice is always obscured by sin and struggles for power. Justice must involve discrimination between competing claims as well as tragic choices between lesser evils. 'A simple Christian moralism counsels people to be unselfish. A profounder Christian faith must encourage men to create systems of justice which will save society and themselves from their own selfishness.'[32] Justice seeks to actively protect from and correct for the social consequences of sin.

According to Niebuhr, the ethic taught by Jesus was a pure love ethic, and thus a purely personal ethic. For Jesus, the 'chief interest was in the quality of life of an individual', and he had a complete 'lack of concern for social and political issues'.[33] Jesus' teachings and example cannot be enacted and should not be attempted at the level of society and nations for several reasons. First, it is too perfectionistic, too much of an ideal.

> There is indeed a very rigorous ethical ideal in the gospel of Jesus, but there is no social ethic in the ordinary sense of the word in it, precisely because the ethical ideal is too rigorous and perfect to lend itself to application in the economic and political problems of our day.[34]

Attempts to enact Jesus' ethic at the level of society and nations will also lead to the same likelihood of success as it did for Jesus, and would thus be irresponsible. Niebuhr wrote that 'an attempt to follow this ideal in the world . . . will inevitably lead us to where it led Jesus, to the cross'.[35]

Jesus' teachings and example also cannot be enacted and should not be attempted at the level of society and nations because Jesus clearly indicated that his way and his teachings were not political. 'He regarded as a temptation the suggestion that he become a political leader or that he develop the political implications of the Messianic idea, and he resisted the effort to make him king.'[36] Thus, while the Anabaptists, Yoder and Niebuhr all make a point of the fact that Jesus refused to be the king some expected him to be, they draw entirely different conclusions from this observation: for the Anabaptists it is a refusal of power which Christians must imitate by not participating in worldly power structures; for Niebuhr it is a refusal of power which proves that it is inapplicable to questions of worldly power structures; and for Yoder it is a redefinition of power in terms of suffering service.

It is easy to read Niebuhr as saying that the ethic of love and the way of Jesus are therefore entirely irrelevant to the social order. However, this is not entirely accurate.

> This does not mean that the ethic of Jesus has no light to give to a modern Christian who faces the perplexing economic and political issues of a technological civilization. It means only that confusion will be avoided if a rigorous distinction is made between a perfectionist and absolute ethic and the necessities of a social situation.[37]

What 'light', then, does the ethic of Jesus give to modern politics? First, the ethic of love is relevant as it stands always in judgement on us; it stands above us as an unattainable ideal to which we must always seek to move closer in our motives and our actions. Love functions as 'an absolute standard by comparison with which all human attainments fall short';[38] it is an ethic which 'we can neither disavow nor perfectly achieve'.[39] It is possible for love to be realized in particular motives of particular individuals; it is possible for love to be approximated in an individual's life; it is entirely impossible for love to govern the social or political. '[A]ny illusion of a world of perfect love without these imperfect harmonies of justice must ultimately turn the dream of love into a nightmare of tyranny and injustice.'[40]

The other 'light' given by the love ethic of Jesus is its ability to make individuals better disciples and citizens, thus reducing the measures of coercive justice required to compensate for their sinfulness.

> The fact that in Jesus the spirit of love flowed out in emulation of God's love, without regard to social consequences, cannot blind the eye to the social consequences of a religiously inspired love. If modern religion were really producing it, it would mitigate the evils of the social struggle.[41]

An entire section (eleven essays) of *Love and Justice* is dedicated to pieces in which Niebuhr argues against pacifism,[42] but his most well-known piece on the subject has been published elsewhere: 'Why the Christian Church Is Not Pacifist'.[43] Niebuhr does not argue that Jesus did not espouse anything like pacifism. On the contrary, he says, 'It is very foolish to deny that the ethic of Jesus is an absolute and uncompromising ethic'.[44] Niebuhr also does not deny that the coming kingdom announced by Jesus is one of peace, but he insists that 'the Kingdom of God is no simple historical possibility. The grace of God for man and the Kingdom of God for history are both divine realities and not human possibilities'.[45]

Instead, Niebuhr's objections to pacifism grow directly from his conclusions on love, justice and the politics of Jesus: the love ethic of Jesus, while 'finally and ultimately normative', is also 'not immediately applicable to the task of securing justice in a sinful world'.[46] On his view, Christian pacifism is a simplistic equation of the Christian gospel with 'the law of love', which mistakes Christianity for having love as its only norm. But Niebuhr insists that Christianity is also marked by an acute awareness of human sinfulness and how it prevents the realization of the ideal of love. 'It believes, in other words, that though Christ is the true norm (the "second Adam") for every man, every man is also in some sense a crucifier of Christ.'[47] With a profound recognition of the depth and consequences of human sinfulness, the Christian comes to see love not as the only normative law but as the 'principle of criticism' which discriminates over and between all forms of and attempts at justice. Thus, love and the kingdom 'hover over every social situation' but are not 'simple alternatives for the present schemes of relative justice'.[48]

According to Niebuhr, pacifism is not only misguided if it holds love as the norm apart from the necessity for justice due to human sinfulness, but it is also in error if it includes suggestions that Christian pacifism can support non-violent resistance to injustice. Because of Niebuhr's passive, selfless definition of love, a 'love ethic' cannot involve any form of active assertions against injustice. Thus, he concludes, 'There is not the slightest support in Scripture for this doctrine of non-violence.'[49] Niebuhr calls the optimistic pacifisms of the nineteenth and early twentieth centuries heresy, because they do not take human sin seriously enough: 'They do not believe that man remains a tragic creature who needs the divine mercy as much at the end as at the beginning of his moral endeavors.'[50] They believe instead that 'just one more sermon on love, and one more challenge to man to obey the law of Christ' will bring peace and end conflict.[51]

Niebuhr does grant that some forms of Christian pacifism are not absolutely heretical, instead they are misguided impulses to Christian perfectionism, 'the impulse to take the law of Christ seriously and not to allow the political strategies, which the sinful character of man makes necessary, to become final norms'.[52] He associates this form with medieval monasticism and with Anabaptism. Importantly, he insists that in both monasticism and Anabaptism, 'the political problem and task were specifically disavowed'.[53] Here we see the political versus apolitical binary resisted by Yoder: because monastics and Anabaptists had a different polity, Niebuhr will not recognize their pacifism as political. This is evident when he argues that pacifists themselves admit that their ethic 'can have no immediate relevance to any political situation; for in every political situation it is necessary to achieve justice by resisting pride and power'.[54]

Was Jesus political? If so, what sort of politics did he practise and teach? Is that political way normative for or applicable to contemporary politics? If so, how? These questions continue to form an important piece of the work of political theology. As we have seen in this chapter, one of the consequences of differing answers to questions surrounding the politics of Jesus is differing attitudes towards the use of violence by Christians. In Chapter 5 we will further explore the questions of justifications for violence and the meaning of Christian peace.

CHAPTER 5

VIOLENCE AND PEACE

It has already become apparent in our explorations thus far that another central issue in political theology is violence. As we saw in Chapter 3, for many violence has been a defining difference between rightfully exercised secular authority and rightfully exercised spiritual authority – the idea that the sword belongs to the government, by the ordination of God. According to most traditional political theologies, one of (if not the central) ordained tasks of human governments is to use coercion, force and violence to keep peace, punish citizens who violate the law and protect citizens and the political body from external threats. This is one aspect of the issue of violence in political theology: is the use of violence and coercive force constitutive of and/or central to the God-given authority and purpose of human government?

We have also seen in Chapter 2 that violence has been a central issue in discussions of the politics of Jesus and the relevance of Jesus to contemporary politics. The moral normativity of Jesus' life and teachings, and the belief that the sword was used only by those outside the perfection of Christ, led the sixteenth-century Anabaptists to absolute pacifism. While John Howard Yoder conceived of the relationship between church and state differently than his Anabaptist ancestors, he also found the non-violence of Jesus to be at the very core of Jesus' moral normativity. Refusing the ways of retaliation and domination is an essential mark of the Christian life and the community which worships Jesus Christ. Reinhold Niebuhr also recognized the non-violent, self-giving love which was the hallmark of Jesus' life and death. However, unlike the Anabaptists or Yoder, Niebuhr concluded that this selfless love was impractical and irrelevant to both the political ordering of societies and the participation of Christians in violent structures and practices which are said to provide societal order. Thus, we have a second aspect of the issue of violence in political theology: in what ways, if any, is the non-violent way of Jesus relevant to contemporary politics?

In Christian ethics, discussions of violence generally focus on arguments for and against just war theory and pacifism.[1] These discussions, while not a primary focus of many who would label their own work as 'political theology', are obviously not irrelevant to the discipline either. The questions of whether or not Christians can ever condone or participate in warfare, and if so under what circumstances, have been subjects of Christian theology from its beginnings. Most scholars agree that the majority of the earliest Christians rejected violence and warfare as means, believing they should not be employed by Christians. We see this in several of the church's earliest theologians. Justin Martyr (100–165) wrote,

> And we who delighted in war, in the slaughter of one another, and in every other kind of iniquity, have in every part of the world converted our weapons of war into implements of peace – our swords into ploughshares, our spears into farmers' implements, and we cultivate piety, justice, brotherly charity, faith, and hope, which we derive from the Father through the crucified Saviour.[2]

Clement of Alexandria (150–215) called the church an army which is without weapons and sheds no blood.[3] Tertullian (160–220) questioned the idea of Christians acting as soldiers.

> Will a son of peace, who should not even go to court take part in battle? Will a man who does not avenge wrongs done to himself have any part in chains, prisons, tortures and punishments? Will he perform guard duty for anyone other than Christ . . . ? . . . By looking around one can see how many other forms of wrongdoing are involved in fulfilling the duties of military camps, things which must be considered violations of God's law . . . [O]nce a man has accepted the faith and has been marked with its seal, he must immediately leave the service.[4]

The pacifist tradition has continued in outposts throughout Christian history, primarily in monasticism and Anabaptism, and in more recent times through movements such as the Catholic Worker Movement, a lay Catholic peace and justice movement started in New York by Dorothy Day in the 1930s.[5] Several contemporary theologians follow Yoder and Stanley Hauerwas in their claims that pacifism is central to Christian ethics and politics, not only as obedience to a duty but as the most faithful way to witness to God's ways in the world.[6]

There are many different types of Christian pacifism, which can be charted across at least two axes. One axis ranges from absolute and categorical rejection of violence to practical or consequentialist rejections of violence. In other words, some pacifists believe that Christians should never engage in violence for any reason because violence itself is wrong, while others argue that the results of violence, particularly in the modern era, are so disastrous as to rule out the use of violence. The other axis ranges from political non-involvement to political activism. In other words, some pacifists believe that rejection of violence requires separation from society either through forming subcultures such as Amish communities or through living within society but refusing to participate in government by voting, holding office or paying the military portion of their taxes. Other pacifists believe that political activism is an essential component of their work as peace-makers and engage in both protest and constructive political work.

However, particularly surrounding the shifts which reconfigured the relationship between Christianity and the Roman Empire, other theologians began to discuss circumstances under which violence might not only be warranted, but morally enjoined upon the Christian. St Ambrose of Milan was among the first theologians to write of the goodness of using force to defend the defenceless. St Augustine argued that Christians could and should employ violence and warfare if the violence was commanded by God or a legitimate human authority, and if it would serve to end or punish cruelty, enmity, rebellion, lust for power and love of violence instead of partaking in them. Given these criteria (though he did not describe them as 'criteria'), 'good men undertake wars, when they find themselves in such a position as regards the conduct of human affairs, that right conduct requires them to act, or to make others act in this way'.[7] These ground rules for Christian participation in war provided by Augustine have come to be thought of as the beginning of Christian just war theory. While the theory of the just war began in Roman philosophy, in Cicero, it was with Ambrose and Augustine that it began to be taken up into Christian theology. It was St Thomas Aquinas who began a more systematic approach, explicitly listing criteria for just wars:

> If a war is to be just, three things are required. First, the authority of the prince by whose command war is to be waged. For it does not pertain to a private person to declare war . . . Second, a just cause is required: that is, those against whom war is to be waged must deserve to have war waged against them because of some wrongdoing . . . Third, it is required that those who wage war should have a righteous intent: that is, they should intend either to promote a good cause or avert an evil.[8]

In the intervening centuries, the just war tradition has continued to be revised and expanded, now usually involving seven to ten criteria. Five to seven of the criteria function to determine whether or not it is just to go to war (*jus ad bellum*) while the remaining two or three serve to govern just behaviour during war (*jus in bello*). More recently, scholars of just war theory have also included discussions of just actions in the ending and aftermath of war (*jus post bellum*).

Many mid-to-late-twentieth-century theologians defended the just war, arguing that the tradition served to restrain and limit the brutality of wars in which states realistically must be expected to engage. In these discussions, the state and/or the international community of states was the moral agent in question, the assumption was that states will engage in wars and the just war tradition serves to limit and restrain them. Recently, however, the conversation has shifted, particularly in the work of second generation political theologian Daniel Bell, who seeks to recover the tradition as more explicitly theological and ecclesiological. He urges just war theorists not only to ask what states should or should not do, but what it means for the church. 'How does our worship, preaching and pastoring, teaching, youth leadership, outreach, daily and weekly interaction, and so on, contribute to making us the kind of people who can abide by the just war discipline?'[9] In this chapter, we will look more closely at a very different approach to just war theory in Jean Bethke Elshtain's *Just War against Terror*, which employs the just war tradition to defend the war in Afghanistan started by the American administration under George W. Bush in 2001.

Before turning to Elshtain, we will look at two other authors on other aspects of the politics of violence and peace. First, we will return to St Augustine. For many just war theorists and Niebuhrian Christian realists, Augustine's work is foundational in demonstrating the necessity of governmental violence and in shaping the Christian just war tradition. Others see in Augustine a vital witness to Christian peace, especially in opposition to the idea that human sociality is fundamentally conflictual and violent. We will also see how Augustine's views on the use of coercion and force changed during his lifetime.

Another vital issue in political theology, especially since the September 11 attacks in America, is evaluation of the widespread discussions of so-called religious violence. There is a familiar narrative in both scholarly and popular circles which attributes most of the world's conflict and warfare to religious disagreements and absolutist assertions. 'Religion' is seen as an inherently dangerous force, and its destructive influence is said to have reached a peak in Europe in the so-called wars of religion in the sixteenth and seventeenth centuries. These wars, so the narrative goes, demonstrated the necessity of the secular state and the division of politics and religion for the maintenance of peace. William T. Cavanaugh calls this narrative a myth, and argues against each of the various aspects of the myth in the book we will explore below.

ST AUGUSTINE (354–430)

At least three different sorts of issues related to violence and peace arise from various discussions and employments of Augustine's political theology. These include the question of whether and when Christians should go to war, the question of the use of violence and coercion against pagans and heretics and the more metaphysical question about the inherent violence or peace of the created order. In addressing the question of war, Augustine is appealed to not only as the first theologian to begin articulating a Christian theology of warfare, but as a constant reminder that from its beginnings the just war tradition has shared with pacifism the conviction that war is sinful and tragic. Jean Bethke Elshtain, whose controversial defence of the recent 'war against terror' will be explored below, says that Augustine's view of war is connected to his view of evil as turning away from the good. 'The fruits of this turning away include a hatred of finitude and a fateful thirst for what might be called a kind of anticreation: a lust to destroy. War is a species of that destruction; hence, war is always a tragedy even "when just."'[10] Thus it is important to remember that all Christian approaches to war which can truly claim St Augustine as forbearer resolutely must be theories of when the tragic use of violence is necessitated by love and justice, not attitudes of either nationalist militarism (which simply and heartily approve whatever wars one's own nation embarks upon) or of crusading holy war (in which war is seen as a good means instead of a tragic means to a good end, and God is seen as 'on our side').

A second issue is the use of violence and coercion against pagans and heretics. Early in his career, Augustine insisted that the church in her own power should use persuasion, argument and pleading to convince and convert heretics. After extensive and painful dealings with the Donatists,[11] Augustine's view was changed. We can see from the argument he made on the subject in *Letter 93* (written in 408) how Yoder might have come to associate Augustine in particular with the lamentable aspects of the Constantinian shift.[12] Augustine wrote that King Nebuchadnezzar is first seen in the book of Daniel compelling believers in God to bow down before idols, and this parallels the situation of Christianity under the unbelieving emperors who persecuted them. Now, however, under believing emperors, the situation of Christians is parallel to that of believers under Nebuchadnezzar after his conversion, when 'he made a decree throughout his empire, that whosoever should speak against the God of Shadrach, Meshach and Abednego, should suffer the penalty which their crime deserved'.[13] Augustine wrote approvingly of the death penalty for pagan 'impiety' and of coercive measures of punishment for heretics carried out by civil authorities. 'For originally my opinion was, that no one should be coerced into the unity of Christ,' he wrote, 'that we must act only by words, fight only by arguments, and prevail by force of reason, lest we should have those whom we knew as avowed heretics feigning themselves to be Catholics. But this opinion of mine was overcome . . .'[14]

In addition to these questions of whether and when use of force was justifiable, there is a more metaphysical question: is the basic sociality of human beings one of conflict and violence or of peace? More broadly, is the ontology of creation – the very nature of its being – violent or peaceful? Some traditions of political theory, both explicitly theological and not, claim a trajectory from Augustine's views on the relationship between human sinfulness and the need for human government to views such as those of Hobbes and Machiavelli which presume a basic human condition of competition and conflict. I have already called this trajectory into question and argued that it is not in fact Augustinian.[15] John Milbank has argued that there is also an ontology of violence in postmodern nihilist philosophy, especially in Friedrich Nietzsche, which should be countered by the ontology of peace found in Augustine.[16]

We have already seen how Augustine described the two cities saying that one had been founded in violence while the other was founded in peace. He was referring specifically to the creation myth of Rome in which Romulus murders his brother Remus in their conflicts over differing plans for the foundation of a city. Having killed Remus, Romulus seeks to establish Rome through abducting hundreds of virgins to populate the city through marriages to Roman men. The women's countrymen take up arms against Romulus. In the heat of battle, Romulus calls upon Jupiter, who intervenes in the war on his behalf. The enemies are driven back then agree to a truce which is the foundation of Rome's peace. Milbank shows that the significance of this creation myth and Augustine's critique of it is not simply that it is an unpleasantly violent story, but that 'The supreme God, therefore, like the founding hero, arises merely as the limiter of a preceding disorder.'[17] Thus the creation of the earthly city is one in which an original state of human conflict and violence is channelled and controlled by further acts of human and divine violence. 'Mythical beginnings of legal order are therefore traced back to the arbitrary limitation of violence by violence, to victory over rivals, and to the usurpation of fathers by sons.' Augustine noted that the statue to the goddess of peace was erected outside Rome's city gates, 'as if to indicate that peace was a benefit brought through war by Rome to others. But if virtue and peace result through war, argues Augustine, the real goddess celebrated by Romans is "foreign injustice" – a "preceding" anarchy and arbitrary domination must always be newly sought out if the founding story is to be again re-enacted'.[18]

By contrast, 'Christians worship the one true God who originates all finite reality in an act of peaceful donation, willing a new fellowship with himself and amongst the beings he has created.' And the heavenly city is where 'angels and saints abide in such a fellowship'.[19] Thus, not only were humans created in and for peace, but within Christianity there is an 'ontology of peace' but no 'ontology of violence'; just as evil is privation in Augustine – a failure to love God in all we are and do – so violence is 'non-being'.[20] As James Smith has summarized Milbank (and Augustine) on this point, 'Violence and oppositional relations are not inscribed into the structure of creation but rather befell creation with the fall . . . [A] specifically Christian onto-logic affirms both a peaceful origin and a peaceful eschaton.'[21] So then, was St Augustine the father of Christian theological defences of war or of Christian peace theology? Was he an advocate of civil coercion and violence on behalf of both church and nation, or was he a compelling critic of the politics of imperial force? He was each and all of these, as is evident in the dizzying array of contrasting and contradictory political theologies which call him their founder, usually by raising one of these features of his thought above the others. Both of the following political theologians, William Cavanaugh and Jean Bethke Elshtain, interact with and draw from Augustine extensively, and yet we will see how their own work on violence varies dramatically from one another's.

WILLIAM T. CAVANAUGH (1962–)

William Cavanaugh is an American, a Roman Catholic and a second generation political theologian. He is currently Senior Research Professor at DePaul University. He wrote his doctorate, which was the basis for his book, *Torture and Eucharist: Theology, Politics and the Body of Christ*,[22] under the supervision of Stanley Hauerwas. His work is characterized by challenges to perceptions of the modern nation-state which have become commonplace in both Christian and wider circles, as well as an emphasis on the Eucharist as a central political practice of the church. Here we will consider his recent book, *The Myth of Religious Violence*.[23]

In Cavanaugh's earlier book, *Theopolitical Imagination*,[24] he briefly argued against the idea that the modern, secular state saved civilization from the inherent violence of religion. Cavanaugh questioned both the historical accuracy of this narrative as well as what he suggested was its alternative soteriology of the state – a false theology in which the state is seen as the saviour of the people. However, *Theopolitical Imagination* was very brief, and critics insisted that such an argument would have to be much more thoroughly presented and evidenced in order to be credible. In *The Myth of Religious Violence*, Cavanaugh provides this more lengthy and fully documented argument.

In naming this myth, Cavanaugh does not question the fact that Christians have committed reprehensible acts of violence. Instead, the myth he challenges is:

> the idea that religion is a transhistorical and transcultural feature of human life, essentially distinct from "secular" features such as politics and economics, which has a peculiarly dangerous inclination to promote violence. Religion must therefore be tamed by restricting its access to public power.[25]

As a second generation political theologian who has been associated primarily with Postliberalism but has also been tangentially involved in Radical Orthodoxy, Cavanaugh is not willing to allow such binaries or assumptions about either the 'religious' or the 'secular' to stand. According to Cavanaugh, 'The problem with the myth of religious violence is not that it condemns certain kinds of violence, but that it diverts moral scrutiny from other kinds of violence. Violence labelled religious is always reprehensible; violence labelled secular is often necessary and sometimes praiseworthy.'[26]

The book is structured around three components of the myth, and Cavanaugh demonstrates how each is mistaken. The first dimension of the myth is that there is something called 'religion' which has existed across time in all human cultures and is separable from other facets of human life such as politics. Cavanaugh shows the difficulty of defining 'religion' in multiple ways. He analyses several recent books on religious violence, demonstrating that their critiques of 'religion' can and should also be applied to many supposedly 'secular' ideologies. 'There is no reason to suppose,' he argues, 'that so-called secular ideologies such as nationalism, patriotism, capitalism, Marxism, and liberalism are any less prone to be absolutist, divisive, and irrational than belief in, for example, the biblical God'.[27] However, the point is not only that 'secular' ideologies can be as violent as 'religious' ones, but that 'the distinction between secular and religious violence is unhelpful, misleading, and mystifying, and it should be avoided altogether'.[28] This conclusion is further argued through an exploration of the historical development of the concept of 'religion' in the West, noting how this development was deeply related to colonialism and the legitimization of the power of the liberal state.[29] Cavanaugh notes that for Augustine and the early and medieval Christianity so deeply shaped by his thought, there was no distinction between 'religious' and 'secular' but between true and false religion.

The second component of the myth is that 'religion' is peculiarly prone to violence and/or that the preponderance of human violence has its genesis in 'religious' impulses. Cavanaugh gives extensive examples from the European wars of the sixteenth and seventeenth centuries which build an argument that these were not always conflicts between groups of differing religious persuasions, nor were 'religious' motives neatly separable from political factors in each specific case.

The final piece of the narrative is that the modern, secular state is the antidote to 'religious violence'. This assertion comes in at least two (often overlapping) forms: the historical claim that the rise of the secular nation-state has saved the West from the chaos of religious wars, and the contemporary claim that the spread of Western, liberal secularism will save the West from the religious violence of Islam. Cavanaugh discusses current narratives of conflict between 'the West and the rest', demonstrating that not only has the secular state failed to free us from the sorts of absolutist, 'us and them' reasoning which many have identified as the root of 'religious' violence, but that the myth currently functions to legitimate precisely such reasoning and absolutism in Western attitudes towards Muslims. This leads in turn to justifications of violence in the name of spreading the goods of modern, secular liberalism.

> In foreign policy, the myth of religious violence serves to cast nonsecular social orders, especially Muslim societies, in the role of villain. *They* have not yet learned to remove the dangerous influence of religion from political life. *Their* violence is therefore irrational and fanatical. *Our* violence, being secular, is rational, peace making, and sometimes regrettably necessary to contain *their* violence. We find ourselves obliged to bomb them into liberal democracy.[30]

As the reader is likely aware, Cavanaugh is referring here especially to shifts in foreign policy particularly in America, but also in Europe, which have occurred in the wake of the attacks of September 11, 2001. He notes how the myth of religious violence serves in this climate both to deepen the caricature of Islam as the root of terrorist violence, and to justify and even glorify Western, state-sponsored violence in response to terrorism – levels and uses of violence which would be difficult to justify apart from the employment of this myth, and certainly difficult to square with the just war tradition. Not all political theologians agree with this assessment of the post-9/11 conflicts, as we will see now in our consideration of Jean Bethke Elshtain's defence of the 'war on terror'.

JEAN BETHKE ELSHTAIN (1941–)

Jean Bethke Elshtain is a Lutheran, a feminist, a political ethicist and a professor at the University of Chicago Divinity School. She earned her doctorate in Politics in the 1970s, and has since published numerous works, both works in the tradition of Public Theology and works which are not explicitly theological. Her theological works seek to build upon the legacies of St Augustine and Reinhold Niebuhr.[31]

In Elshtain's 2003 volume, *Just War against Terror: The Burden of American Power in a Violent World*,[32] she argues for the legitimacy of the US military action in Afghanistan following the September 11 attacks. She makes the theological argument that the debates in America surrounding the 'war on terror' have lacked the realism of Augustine, particularly as read through Niebuhr. According to Elshtain, Americans need to recapture an Augustinian understanding of government. She recalls, 'In the immediate aftermath of September 11, I said to a friend, "Now we are reminded of what governments are for." The primary responsibility of government is to provide basic security – ordinary civic peace.'[33] According to Elshtain, when government does not provide civic peace, 'human life descends to its most primitive level . . . we struggle just to stay alive'.[34] Under good government, there should be no such struggle, as human government exists to protect us from one another. 'The primary reason for the state's existence is to create those minimal conditions that prevent the worst from happening – meaning, the worst that human beings can do to one another.'[35] Here we see Elshtain identifying herself with the form of Augustinianism which has been criticized for its identification with a narrative of original violence.[36] She goes on to argue that the Bush administration was performing just this role of containing violence and enforcing order when entering into the war on terror, and that those intellectuals who oppose the war should be reminded of Niebuhr's criticisms of isolationism and perfectionism in relation to World War II.[37]

Another part of Elshtain's argument is that people should stop reinterpreting radicalism sympathetically; rather we should 'take terrorists at their word'. For Elshtain this means not deflecting scrutiny onto the possible roots of radicalization, but to recognize fully that there are terrorists who very simply hate America and long for its destruction. Where Cavanaugh noted a rising tide of anti-Muslim sentiment as intellectually fashionable since 2001, Elshtain notes this phenomenon but is much more struck by what she identifies as a rising tide of anti-Americanism among European intellectuals. Elshtain echoes the speeches of George W. Bush, claiming that the perpetrators of the September 11 bombings hate America 'because of who we are and what our society represents'. It is not American foreign policy they oppose, 'It is freedom itself that they despise'.[38] She argues that many of the features which characterize the American way of life which is so hated are the freedom, democracy, separation of church and state and gender equality which all grow from Christian conviction and tradition. By contrast, Elshtain suggests, theocracy and war for territorial expansion grow from Muslim conviction and tradition.

> Muhammad was his own Constantine. He established a political order, fusing religious and political power and authority. By contrast, Jesus of Nazareth insisted on a distinction between what is owed to God and what is owed to Caesar. These fundamental differences between two great religions must be recognized. If the Christian distinction has, at times, invited quietism, and a withdrawal from the world, the Islamic tradition has incited engagements with the world that have earned it a reputation as 'the religion of the sword.' Not that Christianity has no knowledge of the sword. But within Christianity the sword always has to justify itself.[39]

Such justification is demonstrated through the use of just war theory, and Elshtain also turns to the specific criteria of just war in defence of the war on terror. Elshtain draws consistently upon Augustine when describing the nature and reasoning of just war theory, emphasizing that it prohibits wars of aggression or aggrandizement and wars which do not aim to establish justice and peace. She also distinguishes just war from *realpolitik*, or political realism – political theories which view power (as opposed to moral or ethical concerns) as the primary concern of governments and international relations. She emphasizes that just war theory shares pacifism's presumption against violence, but parts company with pacifism on the issue of whether or not violence can be a tool for love, peace and justice. She then analyses America's war against terror with reference to each of the just war criteria for going to war (*jus ad bellum*).

The criterion of legitimate authority: '*a war must be openly declared or otherwise authorized by a legitimate authority, so as to forestall random, private, and unlimited violence.*'[40] In some versions of just war theory, this would be two separate criteria: that there must be a declaration of war by a legitimate authority following national and international law, and that there must be a clear announcement of the war (some would say accompanied by clear options for how the war can be prevented – for example withdraw your troops from a specific area by a specific time and we will not strike). According to Elshtain, this criterion was met by the authorization of the US Congress and because the war also fell under the UN Charter Article 51, on self-defence. Others have been critical that the authorization of Congress is not the same as a formal declaration of war (as was issued in the two World Wars, but also was not used in the cases of Korea and Vietnam). And as we will see under the heading of the second criterion, the issue of self-defence is an open question in relation to the just war tradition.

The criterion of just cause: '*a war must be a response to a specific instance of unjust aggression perpetrated against one's own people or an innocent third party, or fought for a just cause.*'[41] In her discussion of this criterion, Elshtain does not note that there is disagreement within Christian just war theories about whether retaliation for an attack is a just cause, the question being under what conditions counter-attack can be classified as self-defence. A particular question in this case would be whether a counter-attack following an act of aggression but fought against a different force on different soil can be classified as an act of self-defence. But Elshtain does not speak in terms of self-defence, as would the majority of the tradition, rather in terms of 'preventing further harm and restoring the preconditions for civic tranquility'.[42] She goes on to note that restoring order after the September 11 attacks was not the only just cause, but that 'love of neighbor' required intervention on behalf of the Afghan people suffering under the Taliban, arguing that 'Afghanistan will be a more just place than if no military action had been taken'.[43]

The criterion of right intent: 'a war must begin with the right intentions.'[44] Elshtain expects her defence of the war in light of the just cause criterion to cover this criterion as well, saying, 'Examining the evidence, we can see that the U.S. military response in Afghanistan clearly meets the just cause criterion of being a war fought with the right intention – to punish wrongdoers and to prevent them from murdering civilians in the future.'[45]

The criterion of last resort: 'a war must be a last resort after other possibilities for redress and defense of the values at stake have been explored.'[46] As her wording of the criterion already reveals, Elshtain interprets 'last resort' in a much less rigorous way than many just war theorists. This criterion usually specifies that non-military options for addressing the problem must have been attempted and exhausted, but Elshtain disagrees.

> Properly understood, last resort is a resort to armed force taken after deliberation rather than as an immediate reaction. The criterion of last resort does *not* compel a government to try everything else in actual fact but rather to explore other options before concluding that none seems appropriate or viable in light of the nature of the threat.[47]

Because Al Qaeda is not a sovereign state, Elshtain argues, there was no 'organized entity to engage',[48] thus negotiation and diplomacy were not possible and peaceful means need not have been pursued. This is perhaps the most tendentious of Elshtain's employments of the criteria of just war theory in relation to its traditional expressions, particularly by Christian theologians.

The criterion of reasonable success: 'do not enter a conflict without reflecting on whether the cause has a reasonable chance of success.[49] Elshtain reserves judgement on this criterion, saying 'I cannot pronounce with any degree of certainty that this criterion is met,' yet in order to ensure it is met, 'it is important for the time being that the United States remain engaged there'.[50] In some versions of just war theory, there is a further criterion *ad bellum*: proportionality. If it is not listed as a separate criterion it is normally considered under the heading of reasonable success; the question is whether the overall good achieved can reasonably be expected significantly to outweigh the total cost in lives, money that could have been spent to help people in other ways and evil which is created by war. In other words, in theological expressions of just war theory in particular, the criterion of success (like the criterion of cause) should have an outward orientation towards the oppressed instead of an inward orientation to national self-interest alone.

Proportionality is usually considered under both headings of *jus ad bellum* and *jus in bello*. Both the decision to go to war and the methods used in war should not be disproportionate to the instigating factor or the methods used by the enemy. There must be a reasonable hope that the action will be proportional before entering into it, and proportionality of means must be exercised during the action. War is a disproportionate response to a minor infraction or minor dispute, and the use of means which kill disproportionate numbers of people or cause other disproportionate damage or harm is considered unjust. For many, this made American talk of 'shock and awe' (rhetoric which arises from a well-formed doctrine which advocates overwhelming military force) inherently questionable.

Elshtain does not address proportionality in her consideration of entering the war in Afghanistan. However she does address proportionality when she turns to the two criteria *in bello*, the criteria which just war theory uses to measure whether a war is just in its actual execution. *The criterion of proportionality: 'the need to use the level of force commensurate with the nature of the threat',*[51] *and the criterion of discrimination: 'the need to differentiate between combatants and noncombatants'.*[52] At the time of her writing in 2003, Elshtain argued that the US military was sufficiently safeguarding against means and abuses which would fall afoul of these criteria.

Many years of continued warfare in Afghanistan have passed since Elshtain wrote *Just War against Terror*, but her estimation of the effort has not been reversed. In an issue of *Christianity Today* in September 2010, she was one of three authors asked to answer the question, 'Should the U.S. stay militarily involved in Afghanistan?' She answered that there was 'no choice'.

> Are we content to watch Afghanistan fall once again under Taliban rule? What on earth do people think would happen if we packed our bags and left the country tomorrow? That we would see the lion lie down with the lamb? We would watch as women now in school were denied an education, and other women were beaten and executed. We would stand by as those who signed on with the prospect of a constitutional Afghanistan are slaughtered. The border with Pakistan, now the site of Taliban operations, would turn into a Taliban stronghold from which they could threaten the security of the entire region. Afghanistan sits astride one of the most dangerous zones in the world. Terrorist entities hanker to generate dirty nuclear weapons with which to threaten all 'infidels,' whether Jews, Christians, or the wrong sort of Muslims. We might pack our bags tomorrow, but we would return as the situation went completely downhill.[53]

Since the first edition of *Just War against Terror*, the invasion of Iraq has also been added to the war against terror. In the 2004 edition of the book, Elshtain adds an epilogue in which she extends her defence of the war on terror to cover the decision of the Bush administration to go to war in Iraq as well.[54] She appeals to Aquinas, saying that the duty to protect the innocent from harm justified this war. She believes and supports George W. Bush's intention of going to war 'to make the world both safer and more just'.[55] She chronicles the abuses of Saddam Hussein, among them 'mass murder' and 'attempted genocide'. She also supports the war as a response to the threat of weapons of mass destruction (WMD), supporting it as an act of pre-emption of employment of WMD.

Most controversial in conversations about the current war in Iraq and just war theory has been the criterion of last resort: can a pre-emptive war ever be considered a last resort? Elshtain defends the invasion as a last resort in reference to the long process of weapons inspections and sanctions, which she claims were not working. And at the time of her writing, she believed the war was also meeting the criteria *in bello*. She concludes, 'I do not see how anyone can look at the evidence and come to any conclusion save that the *in bello* criteria have been met; the real controversy is on the *ad bellum* grounds.'[56]

Just War against Terror closes with a meditation upon the role of America in the international community which is summarized in the book's subtitle, *The Burden of American Power in a Violent World*. This 'burden', as Elshtain understands it, is to be the guarantor of human dignity in a world where human dignity is not secure. 'If human dignity needs a "new guarantee," who will be the guarantor? There is no state except the United States with the power and (we hope) the will to play this role.'[57] This means eschewing American non-involvement policies of the past and being willing to use force to limit force. 'Force that observes limits and is premised on a concern with human dignity is frequently called upon to fight force that operates without limits and makes a mockery of human dignity.'[58]

> Will the U.S. presence in Afghanistan suffice to prevent it from sliding back into tribal warfare or resurgence of Islamist extremism? We do not know. What we do know is that half-measures will not suffice, not in Afghanistan and not in the war against terrorism more generally. Unless America proposes to close itself up behind its borders (something impossible in any case given the porousness of those borders) and revert to isolationism, we can and we must become the leading guarantor of a structure of stability and order in a violent world.[59]

This overview of Elshtain's argument has given us the opportunity to rehearse the criteria of the just war in relation to a particular conflict as well as to see an example of one form of Augustinian political theology which is especially common in America among those who consider themselves Niebuhrian realists. Earlier in this chapter, we saw that Augustine is also employed in very different ways by other political theologians in relation to the issues of peace and violence. Cavanaugh's Augustinianism leads him to call into question modern notions of 'religious' versus 'secular' violence, and Milbank's Augustinianism leads him to call into question the 'ontology of violence', arguing instead that God created the world in and for peace. Notably, for Milbank and many proponents of Radical Orthodoxy, this has not led to pacifist convictions. For

Milbank, our creation in and for peace defines our nature and *telos*, not necessarily all our actions.[60]

Issues of violence and peace permeate political theology, cutting to the core of theologies of the nature of human sociality, government and morality. We have seen in this chapter that the works of Augustine contain and are used to support multiple views of violence and peace; given the space an entire chapter could also be devoted to the use of the Bible by political theologians and Christian ethicists to support widely diverging perspectives on the nature of peace and the use of force. How and whether the Bible and Augustine are employed by various Christians in relation to violence and peace is deeply informed by their theological and ecclesial traditions as well as their schools of thought, as we have seen in the works of Cavanaugh and Elshtain. Elements of the arguments in both Cavanaugh and Elshtain have also made it clear that interfaith issues and the encounter of Christian political theology with other political theologies, particularly from the Islamic tradition, are vital subjects for twenty-first-century political theologians – subjects which unfortunately fall outside the scope of this book. In the following chapter we will further explore one of the other issues touched upon here in our consideration of Cavanaugh – one which has already come to characterize late-twentieth- and early-twenty-first-century political theology: the theological status of liberalism and the liberal nation-state.

CHAPTER 6

LIBERALISM AND DEMOCRACY

Since the 1980s, a persistent theme in political theology (as well as in political theory in general) has been widespread criticism of liberalism as well as defences of liberalism made in response. In this sense of the word, 'liberalism' does not refer to liberal versus conservative politics such as Labour versus Tory or Democrats versus Republicans. In this sense of the word, all these political parties are liberal, and they are the main political parties of two liberal nation-states, the United Kingdom and the United States. Liberalism is the characteristic political philosophy which emerged from the Enlightenment and liberal democracy is now the main form of government in the global North and West. The United States, all states in the European Union, Japan, Mexico, India, South Africa and Canada are considered liberal democracies.

Because liberalism is such a broad umbrella covering a wide variety of political theories, forms and views, it is important both to tease out some of the differences between liberalisms as well as to note the central convictions and commitments which they generally share.[1] At least three distinct forms can be discerned. (1) *Constitutional liberalism* is influenced by the thought of John Locke and Immanuel Kant as well as the social contract theory of Thomas Hobbes. It is associated with the American Revolution (especially Benjamin Franklin and later Thomas Jefferson) and the authors of *The Federalist Papers* (especially Alexander Hamilton and James Madison) as well as the French Revolution (especially Voltaire and Rousseau). This form of liberalism emphasizes the limitation of government size and power in order to prevent abuses of power, concentration of privilege in the hands of the few and the violation of individual rights. (2) *Economic liberalism* is influenced by the thought of John Stuart Mill, Adam Smith and Friedrich von Hayek. It is characterized by the ideology of *laissez-faire* capitalism, including the importance of private property and free markets, and emphasizes free trade internationally and minimal economic intervention by government domestically, as well as individual contract rights. (3) *Welfare liberalism* is influenced by the thought of William Beveridge, John Maynard Keynes and more recently John Rawls. In the United States this form is associated with the New Deal, and in the United Kingdom it is associated with the post-war rise of the welfare state. Welfare liberalism emphasizes the need for economic redistribution, social welfare and civil rights, with a preference for non-coercive means. Where economic liberalism is suspicious of big government, welfare liberalism is suspicious of big business.

Thus, most liberals associate with constitutional liberalism in varying ways, but along with constitutionalism would adopt either economic or welfare liberalism in relation to economic theory and policy. To those more acquainted with contemporary party politics than the history of political theory, economic liberalism and welfare liberalism may seem like opposite ideologies instead of varieties of the same political theory. However, they share the same central concern at their core: the preservation of individual rights. Their differences lie in the fact that some liberal theorists believe that free markets are the best mechanisms for preserving the interests of the individual while other liberal theorists believe that government-directed redistribution is the best mechanism.

Robert Song has noted five 'family resemblances' which bind together such disparate political perspectives into one theory. (1) Liberalism has a particular view of human agency; it views the individual as a detached, sovereign chooser. (2) Liberalism has a particular ethics which focuses on individual moral autonomy and is guided by the distinction between facts and values. (3) Liberalism is a school of thought marked by three main characteristics: individualism (in ethics, in religious choice, in consent to government and in economics); universalism (in that it broadens categories of what and who is relevant, and in that it believes it can make generalizations which hold in all times and places); and abstraction (liberal principles must be abstract in order to be universal).

(4) Liberalism is committed to a form of rationality in which disputes are settled through reason instead of violence, and reason is instrumental for the pursuit of individual gain. (5) Liberalism's view of history is that it has been and will continue to be a story of human progress.

As we saw in Chapter 2, most theologians in the first generation of twentieth-century political theology considered themselves critical friends of modernity. This included liberal politics. They were critical of some specific features or particular outworkings of modern liberalism, but most assumed that the liberal state was either a neutral reality which one could assume or a positive development which should be (mostly) embraced. In the following generation, political theologians became more critical of modernity and liberalism.[2] While Postliberal Theology is given its title primarily for its rejection of theological liberalism, most Postliberal Theologians are also critics of political liberalism. Radical Orthodoxy has also included a critique of liberalism. However, it is important to note that while second generation political theologians do tend to be more unreservedly critical of modernity and liberalism than the first generation, they should not be understood as 'antimodern'. James Smith's comments on this aspect of Radical Orthodoxy (RO) are also applicable to Postliberal critics of modernity and liberalism such as Hauerwas: 'To be antimodern in the sense of Protestant fundamentalism is to be the simple negation of modernity and hence still within a modern paradigm. RO is critical of modernity in a way that seeks to circumvent its assumptions.'[3] Or as Milbank has put it, 'Radical Orthodoxy, although it opposes the modern, also seeks to save it. It espouses, not the pre-modern, but an alternative version of modernity.'[4]

Many of the characteristics of liberalism seem straight-forwardly positive; aren't democracy, freedom, reason and progress good things to emphasize? Why, then, might so many political theologians today find fault with liberalism? There are at least four aspects of modern liberalism which political theologians (and many political theorists) reject. One is its ethical orientation, which is towards procedure and duty (following the deontological ethics of Immanuel Kant) instead of towards the ethical *telos* or the good (as in Aristotelian and/or Hegelian ethics). Another problem is the liberal concept of the self, which imagines the human individual as autonomous, unencumbered and freely choosing, while critics of this view emphasize that as humans we are historically situated, conditioned, communally obligated and limited. This also relates to the third aspect, the basic unit of government. For liberalism, the basic unit under discussion is the individual, the state or civil society; critics believe it should be the locality, community or world. Finally, modern liberalism is marked by universalism in the sense that it rests on the conviction that norms and practices such as 'justice' and 'rights' can have universal meaning and application. Critics of liberalism are sceptical of abstract, universal claims and emphasize the importance of particularity and historicity.

Two specific systems or features of modern liberalism which are often part of contemporary discussions are modern liberal democracy and human rights. Some critics of modern democracy assume that democracy is the best available form of government but go on to argue that modern liberal democracy cannot be or is not currently functioning as a true democracy. Another line of critique questions whether or not democracy is indeed the best form of government. Likewise, critical questions about human rights may focus on whether the practical outworking matches the positive aspirations of the human rights tradition (as in Liberation Theology's questions about whether the current human rights system primarily serves the interests of the most privileged members of the global society instead of the most vulnerable), or on whether the aspirations of human rights arise from philosophically dubious perspectives such as individualism and universalism.

Readers not familiar with these debates may find themselves wondering what the alternatives to modern liberal democracy might be. Some critics of modern liberal democracy harken back to premodern politics, either to advocate premodern forms of democracy (this mainly involves advocacy of smaller-scale politics, as ancient democracy was of the city-state instead of the nation-state), to early modern forms of liberalism (as in Oliver O'Donovan's advocacy of early modern Christendom), or to premodern versions of monarchy. Others may advocate other modern political theories and forms. The most prominent modern alternative to liberalism, totalitarianism, is (thankfully) rarely defended by either political theorists or theologians! However, another alternative, which may take premodern, modern or postmodern forms, is collectivism (including various forms of socialism and communism). Where liberalism focuses first on the rights of the individual, collectivism begins with the good of the community. Communitarianism, one form of collectivism, has been advocated in the late-twentieth and early-twenty-first centuries by many critics of liberalism.

While these criticisms of and alternatives to modern liberalism can be (and are) offered by thinkers outside the theological disciplines, there are also particularly Christian reasons why these critiques resonate with political theologians. In the remainder of this chapter we will consider two of the most prominent contemporary theological critics of liberalism, Stanley Hauerwas and John Milbank. We will then turn to a recent constructive argument for a contemporary Augustinian liberalism, in Eric Gregory's *Politics and the Order of Love*.

STANLEY HAUERWAS (1940–)

Famously born in Texas and raised in the Methodist Church, Stanley Hauerwas went on to study at Yale Divinity School and to teach at the University of Notre Dame and Duke Divinity School. He is a Postliberal Theologian whose work is deeply influenced by the thought of Karl Barth, John Howard Yoder and Alasdair MacIntyre. His theological and ecclesial impulses are both deeply Catholic and markedly Anabaptist, and he has been influential in introducing the possibility and contributing to the popularity of engagement between these two theological traditions which have often been treated as opposites.[5]

A critique of liberalism, especially in the American context, has been a central feature of Hauerwas's work throughout his career. We will look here at two early essays which introduce the criticisms of liberalism which have continued to recur in his work. 'A Christian Critique of Christian America' was written in 1986 in response to the rise of the New Christian Right in America.[6] In it, Hauerwas argued that liberal Christians' annoyance at figures such as Jerry Falwell did not stem from their ideological differences, but from the fact that Falwell and others had merely bought into the same liberal agenda they had been pushing for decades, but had done so in a very different way than they had hoped. 'The Church and Liberal Democracy' was first published in 1981 and focused on the consequences of liberalism for Christian social ethics in America.[7] These two essays are specifically on the topic of liberalism, but as John Berkman noted in his introduction to *The Hauerwas Reader*, 'Hauerwas eagerly confronts the problematic assumptions of liberalism in many if not most of his essays', including ones on the Holocaust, the family, the mentally handicapped, sexual ethics, medicine, abortion, sexual orientation and character formation.[8]

Hauerwas provides a narrative of liberalism in America and its role in American churches and American Christian ethics. He notes that 'America, more than any nation before or after, has been the product of a theory of government'.[9] In other words, America has the unique distinction of being the nation which was born at the height of optimism and confidence in the new ideas of modern liberal democracy; it came into existence as an experiment in these ideas and ideals. In that sense, modern liberal democracy is more part of the American DNA, as it were, than any other nation's. In relation to the founding philosophy of America, Hauerwas specifically focuses on Hobbes and Locke, who both 'to be sure in very different ways, viewed the political problem as how to get individuals, who are necessarily in conflict with one another, to enter into a cooperative arrangement for their mutual self-interest'.[10] Liberalism's roots in Hobbes and Locke give rise to two main problems, according to these essays: the location of authority in the individual, and the establishment of self-interest as the foundation of the social order. Fast-forward to the turn of the twentieth century, and we see the enshrinement of liberalism in the formation of the ethical discourse of American Protestantism. Through the influence of Walter Rauschenbusch and the Social Gospel Movement, mainline Protestants embraced the idea that their social-ethical duty was to 'Christianize' the social order, that social structures needed to be 'saved', and that the redemption of social orders came through democratization.[11] Eventually, the majority ethos of American Protestantism would be marked by the conviction that modern liberal democracy and Christianity were mutually implicated; to support one was to support the other.

Hauerwas also traces this trajectory through the influence of Reinhold Niebuhr. Though he was critical of the Social Gospel, it was primarily because of its optimism in human nature not its embrace of modern liberal democracy, and part of the optimism of the Social Gospel was its emphasis on the role of love in transforming the political order. Yet in rejecting the ethic of love in politics,[12]

Niebuhr did not dampen American Protestantism's enthusiasm for social transformation. 'Reinhold Niebuhr took the enthusiasm of the social gospel and made it all the more powerful by suggesting the limits of what love could accomplish through the politics characteristic of our society', because in Niebuhr, 'those limits do not lessen the Christian duty to use power to secure the forms of justice possible in our social and political system'.[13] In fact, the exercise of power to promote justice is the way to be 'responsible' in the Niebuhrian realism that was so thoroughly embraced in Protestant social ethics. However, this trajectory has not been limited to American Protestantism, according to Hauerwas, but was also taken up within American Catholicism under the influence of John Courtney Murray, who sought both to 'make America amenable to Catholic social theory' as well as to 'make Catholics amenable to America' through his work on natural law in relation to church, state and society.[14]

The next important figure in this trajectory of American Christianity's enmeshment with modern liberal democracy – a trajectory perhaps most evident in the political theology of the Public Theologians – is the influence of John Rawls' theory of justice. In *A Theory of Justice* (1971), Harvard philosopher Rawls argued that justice is fairness, and fairness can be spelled out in principles to which all rational individuals would agree given a fair and equal position. This fair and equal position – the 'original position' which is not unrelated to the 'state of nature' of earlier liberal thought – was illustrated by Rawls through a thought experiment: what if a body of people which equally represented a society could gather together to form a social contract under a 'veil of ignorance' which would hide from them their own and others' special interests, station in life and future possibilities? Their natural self-interest would guide them towards principles of justice which were as fair to everyone as possible, because anyone's interests might be their own. For Rawls, this theory leads to two principles of justice, liberty and difference, which focus on equal access to opportunity and the minimization of social and economic inequality.[15]

Hauerwas argues that while remaining committed to the disestablishment of religion, liberal American Christians also remain committed to 'Christianizing' the social order, albeit with a dose of realism from Niebuhr's theological anthropology, and that they understand 'Christianizing' primarily in terms of 'justice'. 'That such is the case helps explain the enthusiasm for the work of John Rawls among those working in Christian ethics.'[16] Christianization of society came to be understood widely as working for equality of opportunity for individuals and redistribution of wealth. 'Rawls thus becomes the language of common grace that continues the project of Christianizing America.'[17]

As Hauerwas traces this narrative and moves to call it into question, we see four distinct themes of his critique of liberalism. First, according to Hauerwas, liberalism is not well-suited to making us good humans. One reason for this is that it is ahistorical and 'storyless'. The formative power of narrative is a central theme in Hauerwas's work, especially in the 1980s and 1990s, and one of his objections to liberalism is its rejection of the story-formed nature of human character. By holding the authority of the unencumbered, free and autonomous choosing individual at its heart, liberalism is committed to the idea that history and tradition (the stories which form us) are at best irrelevant and at worst dangerous. 'Our assumption [as Americans] has been that, unlike other societies, we are not creatures of history, but that we have the possibility of a new beginning. We are thus able to form our government on the basis of principle rather than the arbitrary elements of a tradition.'[18] The ahistorical nature of liberalism is closely tied to another reason it does not make us good humans, which is its neglect of virtue. Not only is a common history lacking, but also a common good, and 'liberalism provided a philosophical account of society designed to deal with exactly that problem: A people do not need a shared history; all they need is a system of rules that will constitute procedures for resolving disputes as they pursue their various interests'.[19] In other words, when the freedom of the individual becomes the driving force instead of the common good, the concern is only for the best principles and procedures for achieving maximum individual freedom instead of the convictions and practices which form virtuous people.

> Americans, as is often contended, are good people or at least want to be good people, but our problem is that we have lost any idea of what that could possibly mean. We have made 'freedom of the individual' an end in itself and have ignored the fact that most of us do not have the slightest idea of what we should do with our freedom.[20]

Of course, modern liberals share one concept of what we should do with our freedom: consume. 'The genius of liberalism was to make what had always been considered a vice, namely unlimited desire, a virtue.'[21] For Hauerwas, liberalism's embrace of the market 'as the dominant institution of society' was an inevitable outcome of its Hobbesian notion of self-interest and its rejection of virtue and the common good, 'for in a social order where distrust is primary we can only rely on abundance and technology to be a substitute for cooperation and community'.[22]

Although this is by no means a primary concern for Hauerwas, as we will see, it is also a part of his critique of modern liberal democracy that it is not well-suited to making us good citizens. Our optimism about democracy, says Hauerwas, lulls us into a false sense that we actually govern ourselves. 'Democracy is still government by the elite,' he notes, 'though it may be less oppressive since it uses language in its justification that provides ways to mitigate oppressiveness'.[23] The ability of citizens in modern liberal democracies to be lulled into this false optimism is directly related to the ahistorical philosophy of liberalism. Because liberalism 'continues to promise us new tomorrows of infinite creation', we are ironically limited and determined by our conviction that we are entirely free. '[T]he more we are convinced we are free, the more determined we become.'[24] Instead of freeing us to become good citizens, the liberal ideology of freedom may blind us to how unquestioningly beholden we are to the nation-state.

> The story that liberalism teaches us is that we have no story, and as a result we fail to notice how deeply that story determines our lives. Accordingly, we fail to recognize the coercive form of the liberal state, as it, like all states, finally claims our loyalty under the self-deceptive slogan that in a democracy the people rule themselves because they have 'consented' to be so ruled. But a people who have learned the strenuous lesson of God's lordship through Jesus' cross should recognize that 'the people' are no less tyrannical than kings or dictators.[25]

The main focus of Hauerwas's critique, closely related to the first two lines of criticism, is that wedding Christianity to liberalism does not make good Christians or faithful churches. Hauerwas echoes Yoder's line on Constantinianism,[26] and names the identification of liberal democracy with Christianity as America's particular form of Constantinianism. 'I am convinced that this habit of thought, which Yoder calls Constantinianism, must be given up. Otherwise, we Christians remain caught in the same habits of thought and behavior that implicitly or explicitly assume that insofar as America is a democracy she is Christian.'[27] This assumption is tied to another, that 'the destiny of a particular state and social order was intrinsic to God's Kingdom'.[28] Instead, according to Hauerwas, the only polity central to the kingdom of God and worthy of the loyalty demanded by the liberal nation-state is in fact the church. 'The challenge is always for the church to be a "contrast model" for all polities that know not God. Unlike them, we know that the story of God is the truthful account of our existence, and thus we can be a community formed on trust rather than distrust.'[29] The church's social and political task is not to shore up the liberal state but 'to be an alternative polity', which means virtuous formation of communities which 'should be the source for imaginative alternatives for social policies that not only require us to trust one another, but chart forms of life for the development of virtue and character as public concerns'.[30]

Hauerwas's concern here for the church as an 'alternative polity' to imagine 'alternatives for social policies' and open possibilities for 'virtue and character as public concerns' is important to note. His critics remain convinced that Hauerwas calls for the withdrawal of Christians from public and political life into the sectarian ghetto of Christian community. In both these essays, Hauerwas seeks to forestall this conclusion. 'Am I suggesting that Christians must "withdraw" from the social, political, and legal life of America? I am certainly not arguing that; rather, I am trying to suggest that in order to answer questions of "why" or "how" Christians participate in the life of this country we do not need a theory about the Christian character of democracy.'[31] Put another way, 'This does not involve a rejection of the world, or a withdrawal from the world; rather it is a reminder that the church must serve the world on her own terms . . . The first task of the church is to exhibit in our common life the kind of community possible when trust, and not fear, rules our lives.'[32]

JOHN MILBANK (1952–)

I once heard Stanley Hauerwas asked if he and John Milbank had such strong theological affinities and similarities that they could be understood as doing the same sort of theology – as sharing a theological project. He responded that he was not sure they were doing the same thing so much as making the same enemies. Milbank, sitting next to him, nodded. In the case of their critiques of modern liberalism and democracy, this rings true. They are equally opposed by defenders of liberalism, modern democracy and human rights for their similar critiques, yet in their constructive responses in particular, they have significant differences. Some of these differences stem from their differing biographies. Hauerwas is American, Methodist (most of his life) and Postliberal, while Milbank is British, Anglican and is the founding thinker of Radical Orthodoxy. He has taught at the University of Virginia and the University of Cambridge, and is currently a professor at the University of Nottingham.

Here we will look primarily at Milbank's essay, 'Liberality versus Liberalism' (2008),[33] which was written in response to the neoliberal politics of the Bush administration in the United States and New Labour in the United Kingdom. This essay will be considered in conjunction with his landmark work, *Theology and Social Theory* (1990), which set out the programme which he has continued in his subsequent work.

Milbank agrees that the self-understanding of citizens of liberal democracies can lull them into being deceived about how free and democratic their societies are. Referring to the Bush administration in America and the war in Iraq joined by his own nation, Milbank noted, 'recent events demonstrate that liberal democracy can itself devolve into a mode of tyranny'.[34] He is also sceptical about 'human rights' as conceived within the modern, liberal mode. '[A]n appeal to "human rights" as an unassailable norm will always mean in reality a covert allowance of specific freedoms for some and certain converse inhibitions of specific freedom for others for interested reasons of power-politics.'[35] He is critical of the founding philosophy of liberalism, especially as related to the social contract, and criticizes 'the central premises of liberalism which, as Pierre Manent says, are based in Manichean fashion upon the ontological primacy of evil and violence: at the beginning is a threatened individual, piece of

property, or racial terrain'.[36] And he questions liberalism's economics, in both free-market and welfare forms, calling the mistake of
current politics the assumption that 'the "free market" is a given
which should either be extended or inhibited and balanced. For if
the upshots of the free market are intrinsically unjust, then "cor-
recting" this through another welfare economy is only a mode of
resignation; moreover its task is Sisyphean and periodically doomed
to go under with every economic downturn'.[37] In these and many
other ways, Milbank's criticisms of modern liberalism resonate with
Hauerwas's questions about its philosophy, ethics and politics.

Beyond the similarities of their critiques, however, their constructive responses to liberalism are significantly different. Hauerwas
employs Aristotelian virtue ethics and Yoderian theology to describe
how the church should be an alternative body politic not shaped by
the assumptions and errors of liberalism but by the politics of Jesus.
He resolutely refuses to offer an alternative vision of the state (or
other form of secular polity), insisting this is not the task of theologians. Instead, he maintains that the primary concern for Christian
ethics (and political theology) is for the church to become more
truly the polity she is meant to be. Milbank is in agreement that
the church is the true polity. According to him, where Christianity
has been wedded to liberalism, the church has been regarded 'as
simply a spiritual association of souls' instead of a political body.[38]
Whereas, '[a]ll "political" theory, in the antique sense, is relocated
by Christianity as thought about the Church'.[39] However, where
Hauerwas issues his call for 'the church to be the church' primarily through Yoder, Milbank comes to the church as true polity
through Augustine, noting that 'as a *civitas* [city], the Church is, for
Augustine, itself a "political" reality'.[40]

Unlike Hauerwas, Milbank's interest is less in the church being
a counter-polity than in both polities of church and state being in
analogous forms derived from classical philosophy and Christian
theology. For example, he turns to a Pauline theology of the body
of Christ to describe how his understanding of sovereignty and
representation differs from the social contract theory of the sovereign's power arising from the consent of the governed:

> Beyond this it needs to be supposed that truth lies with the
> people somewhat in the way that truth lies in the Church for
> St Paul . . . The people give their goods to the head of the Church

who is Christ; in like manner the people should give their gifts of insight and talent to the sovereign representative who acts in their name.[41]

He also stresses the importance of boundaries between church and state not being impermeable; in fact they should be 'extremely hazy, so that a "social" existence of many complex and interlocking powers may emerge, and forestall either a sovereign state, or a statically hierarchical church'.[42]

This means that Milbank does not hesitate to prescribe parameters for the best form of government, where Hauerwas steadfastly insists that theories of the state are not within the tasks of Christian theology. Milbank endorses a complex mixture of democracy, aristocracy, monarchy and socialism which arises from an equally complex mixture of Aristotelianism, Platonism, Stoicism, Augustinianism, Thomism and Catholic Social Teaching. In his political theology – and the wider project of Radical Orthodoxy, as its name indicates – this mixture creates theory which is at once radical and traditional. One could read some bits of Milbank and think him a radical new form of socialist, as in this excerpt where he names the destructive consequences of liberalism:

> The 'modernity' of liberalism has only delivered mass poverty, inequality, erosion of freely associating bodies beneath the level of the state and ecological dereliction of the earth – and now, without the compensating threat of communism, it has abolished the rights and dignity of the worker, ensured that women are workplace as well as domestic and erotic slaves, undermined working-class family structure, and finally started to remove the ancient rights of the individual which long precede the creed of liberalism itself (such as *habeas corpus* in Anglo-Saxon law) and are grounded in the dignity of the person rather than the 'self-ownership' of the autonomous liberal man (*sic*).[43]

One could read other bits of Milbank and think him an unreconstructed premodern, as in this excerpt where he insists that democracy must be balanced by aristocracy and monarchy:

> Democracy, which is the 'rule of the Many,' can only function without manipulation of opinion if it is balanced by an

'aristocratic' element of the pursuit of truth and virtue for their own sake on the part of some people whose role is legitimate even if they remain only 'the Few,' although they should ideally be themselves the Many. Democracy equally requires the 'monarchic' sense of an architectonic imposition of intrinsic justice by a transcendent 'One,' however constituted, that is unmoved by either the prejudices of the Few or those of the Many.[44]

What seems to make his work inscrutable to many of his critics is that both these elements exist within his political theology, and in interdependence instead of in tension with one another. In fact, the interdependence of radicalism and elements of the classical and Christian traditions is central to his project: '[W]e need to take the risk of thinking in an altogether new way that will take up the traditions of socialism less wedded to progress, historical inevitability, materialism, and the state, and put them into debate with conservative anti-capitalist thematics and the traditions of classical and biblical political thought . . .'[45] For Milbank, the key themes of these traditions include gift-exchange in contrast to contract theory and market capitalism, the primacy of love and charity in contrast to self-interest and competition and sacramentalism (the goodness and sacredness of all God's creation) in contrast to utilitarianism and instrumentalism (the goodness only of what 'works' and is 'useful'). This trajectory also points towards a shift in focus away from the national both inward towards the local and outward towards the global. '. . . Christian principles of polity stand totally opposed to any idea of the "nation-state" as the ultimate unit and rather favour at once the natural pre-given "region" on the one hand, and the universal human cosmopolis on the other.'[46]

Readers unfamiliar with Milbank's writing or his sources may be put off initially by his employment of 'aristocracy' and 'hierarchy' – words which liberalism has taught us are vestiges of the oppressive, pre-liberal past. We should note, however, that Milbank is not using these terms in their popular senses, but as they arise from the classical and Christian traditions, especially Plato and Aquinas. In this sense, the aristocracy is not the class of Lords of the manor, privileged by disproportionate wealth and land ownership. It is rather the idea that a society should have at least some people, if only the few, whom the society commits to support in a life dedicated to education and excellence, and to listen and learn from the different perspective and wisdom unique to lives so formed. We should also note that when Milbank explicitly embraces hierarchy through advocating aristocracy and monarchy alongside democracy, he is not suggesting that egalitarian liberal societies should reintroduce hierarchy where there is none. Rather he wants us to recognize the 'hierarchies of liberalism', which are competitive and utilitarian (and thus destructive of the common good) while classical, 'spiritual' hierarchy is 'constantly self-cancelling' instead of competitive (e.g. teachers willingly give way as their pupils become the next generation of teachers) and has its *telos* in excellence instead of looking only for utility. I do not suggest, of course, that these clarifications will prevent all readers from being put off by Milbank's political theology, which continues to be highly controversial among both those who do and do not understand it accurately.

POLITICS AND THE ORDER OF LOVE (2008)

One contemporary scholar who remains unconvinced by Milbank is Eric Gregory, Professor of Religion at Princeton University. His book, *Politics and the Order of Love*, is perhaps the most prominent example of a recently published defence of liberalism. In a revised version of his doctoral thesis written under Gene Outka at Yale University, he argues for a reinvigorated Augustinian liberalism. 'Liberal democracy is not the defeat of Christian witness,' he contends. 'To the contrary, the achievements of the liberal tradition can be cast as triumphs of a long history of Christian social and political theory.'[47]

According to Gregory, 'the continuing debate over modern liberalism has to a large extent consisted in variations on Augustinian themes and antiphonal responses to them'. In fact, he claims, it 'would not be a great exaggeration to see these debates as a series of footnotes to Augustine'.[48] And yet, for Gregory, the way forward is not necessarily to determine precisely what Augustine said and meant; political theology will not resolve its attitude towards modern liberalism through a 'quest for the historical Augustine', as modern liberalism was unimaginable for him. Instead, the debate should be about better and worse forms of liberalism. Gregory distances himself both from Augustinian theologians who reject political liberalism (especially Milbank) and political liberals who reject Augustinian theology (especially Hannah Arendt), then he moves to present the type of Augustinian liberalism which he considers the most fruitful.

He describes how there has been a historical progression through which three distinct types of Augustinian liberalism arose in the twentieth century. First was the Augustinian realism of Reinhold Niebuhr which, in response to the optimism and enthusiasm of both theological liberalism and pre-war liberal democracy, brought the Augustinian doctrine of original sin to the forefront. This theological emphasis was wedded with the political realism of Machiavelli and the sociology of Max Weber, and as we have seen, became extremely influential in American Protestantism in particular and has remained the dominant form of Augustinian liberalism. Gregory defines the operative virtue in this stream of liberalism as hope, 'particularly eschatological hope that transcends the tragedies and tensions of politics'.[49] However, it is the tragedies and tensions which are more determinative for Augustinian realists and, according to Gregory, this form of Augustinian liberalism is limited by its focus on politics as the restraint of evil and by the resulting moral consequentialism.

Gregory identifies a second distinct form of Augustinian liberalism, Augustinian proceduralism, arising in the 1970s and 1980s in response to the work of John Rawls. This variety emphasizes the importance of justice, fairness and respect in the pluralistic conditions of liberal societies. Accordingly the central virtue of this school is justice, understood in Rawlsian terms. Gregory's assessment of this school of thought is that while its vision of politics is less limited and more positive than Niebuhr's, its conception of justice is too minimalist and results in virtues important to politics being relegated to the private sphere.

In the 1990s a third variety, Augustinian civic liberalism, emerged in the work of theologians such as Jean Bethke Elshtain and Oliver O'Donovan. For Gregory, the most significant roots of this tradition are in the work of Martin Luther King Jr. It is characterized by the Augustinian perspective that 'human beings and the societies they form are best understood in terms of the loves they embody and express',[50] thus its distinguishing virtue is love. This is the version of Augustinian realism with which Gregory identifies himself, arguing that it corrects the other two through its emphasis on love of God and neighbour. 'Indeed, one conclusion of this book is that Martin Luther King Jr, not Reinhold Niebuhr, is the great Augustinian liberal of modernity.'[51]

These three types of Augustinian liberalism share in common a liberal affirmation of secularity and an Augustinian emphasis on politics as limited and corruptible. These core similarities are also embraced by Gregory. 'I affirm aspects of this modern tradition, notably what is today called the separation of church and state supporting a constitutional regime of check and balances. I also affirm its capacity to deflate moral and political pretension.'[52]

However, Gregory also seeks to amend and augment the tradition, especially in relation to the third, civic form. One aspect of this augmentation comes through the virtue tradition. Here Gregory sees the task to 'reconstruct a kind of *Augustinian civic virtue* that might in turn encourage a more ambitious political practice', and 'offer a vision of citizenship open to social transformation by attending to virtue'.[53] Along with a focus on virtue, Gregory seeks to strengthen this tradition by putting it into conversation with feminist political theory, taking seriously their objections both to aspects of liberalism and to Augustinianism.[54] However, Gregory's augmentation of Augustinian civic liberalism does not come from philosophy and political theory alone, but is substantively theological. He distinguishes his own liberalism from its most prevalent forms, saying, '*Christology and neighbour-love* rather than *theism and self-love* are the central conceptual terms for any Augustinian liberalism that wants to be theological'.[55] And where most Augustinian liberalisms focus on Book 19 of *City of God*, where Augustine explicitly addresses matters of government, war and peace, Gregory's Augustinian liberalism focuses elsewhere: 'Book 10 of the *City of God* is the basic text for Augustinian politics: the heart of Augustine's account of the true worship of the crucified God and the charitable service of neighbour in collective *caritas*.'[56]

When Augustinian civic liberalism arose, so also was a fourth type of contemporary Augustinianism coming into focus, but this was the antiliberal Augustinianism found especially in Radical Orthodoxy which echoed many of the criticisms also being voiced by Stanley Hauerwas. Gregory notes from the outset of his book that Hauerwas and Milbank are the two most prominent and articulate theological critics of liberalism against whom he will need to defend his proposal.

> Two of the most energetic and provocative programs in theological ethics today, laying claim to the Augustinian tradition, have declared Niebuhrianism a theological and political failure. These movements associate *any* defense of political liberalism with failures of theological liberalism and secular nihilism. Against John Milbank and Stanley Hauerwas, I do not share this view. Theological orthodoxy and political liberalism are not alternative answers to the same question.[57]

However, Gregory also is in agreement with many of the specific objections raised by Hauerwas and Milbank. He agrees with their grim diagnosis of the present state of liberal democracy, referring to the 'depressing realities of liberal democracies marked by dramatic political and economic inequalities',[58] as well as 'the increasing self-absorption displayed in a rights-governed and consumer-oriented liberal culture'.[59] He agrees that forms of liberalism which degenerate into a 'never-ending story about politics as a response to sin' are insufficient.[60] In fact, he does not defend a traditionless, storyless liberalism; rather he consistently presents both Augustinianism and liberalism as traditions and particular sorts of narratives with histories. He agrees that political theology should not allow for the 'reduction of politics to state-centered government activity',[61] and that Niebuhr's employment of Augustine failed to recognize 'the Augustinian claim that church (not state) is itself a historical, sacramental reality'.[62] He recognizes ways in which Augustinian liberalism has gone wrong, noting that proponents 'can justify all manner of injustice in the name of two kingdoms, regretful responsibility and "dirty hands." Lutheran streams of Augustinian politics are particularly vulnerable to this temptation, evident most recently in theological justifications of the use of torture to combat terrorism'.[63] He also agrees that part of the answer is a recovery of the virtue tradition. In short, political liberalism as 'a demythologized notion of original sin as a basis for anti-utopian foreign and domestic policy' simply is not good enough.[64] Gregory expects more from liberalism than 'the creation of a space where we do not kill each other and we do not interfere with the conditions of economic exchange'.[65] He summarizes his similarities and differences with Hauerwas and Milbank by saying that his

> . . . effort to free Augustine from Niebuhrian realism does not altogether abandon Niebuhr, and it still remains at odds with

Hauerwas and Milbank. But my development of Augustinian Christology complements their effort to recast political theology in terms of the perfections of Christian virtue, although it is not built on the back of antiliberalism.[66]

For our purposes, two aspects of Gregory's constructive proposal should be highlighted.[67] First, according to Gregory, political morality goes wrong through overemphasizing either love or sin. Where there is too much confidence in love, one finds 'arrogant perfectionism'. Where there is too much suspicion due to sin, one finds 'negative liberalism'. 'The error of both views is a failure to relate love and sin to each other in ways that constrain both appeals.'[68] Thus, the 'dynamic relation between love and sin' is the strength of Augustinian civic liberalism as Gregory presents it.

The other crucial lynchpin for Gregory is his understanding of secularity. For him, the most forceful criticism of liberalism waged by Yoder, Hauerwas and Milbank is 'the refusal to ally Christian social ethics with liberalism because of its hegemonic commitment to secularism'.[69] However, Gregory means to defend secularity without promoting secularism; he 'distinguishes Augustine's desacralization of politics from the bifurcation of politics and the aspirations of virtue'.[70] In the following excerpt, Gregory clarifies his use of 'secularity' and 'desacralization'.

> Every Augustinian liberal affirms secularity as a shared time afforded all humanity by the common grace of God. This affirmation, following Augustine's overcoming an initial attraction to imperial theology of the Constantinian establishment, rejects the sacralization of earthly political communities as vehicles of salvation. This move serves as the crucial element that opens the door for a separation of the political and the ecclesial without separating morality from politics or condemning the religious to private subjectivity.[71]

Gregory differentiates this from secularism, the advocacy of a secular sphere which is free from religion, transcendence, metaphysics and matters of personal value and morality. It is this secularism which Milbank not only rejects, but denies the possibility of its existence. 'Here, I think, is the nub,' writes Gregory. 'Milbank identifies the "secular" with immanence and the denial of transcendence. On these terms, it is impossible to offer an ambivalent assessment of liberal democracy . . . No doubt many citizens committed to liberal democracy are committed to secularism. But why should Milbank take one version of the liberal story to be the whole story?'[72] In opposition both to liberals who promote secularism and to antiliberals who oppose liberalism for its promotion of secularism, Gregory identifies himself (on this point) with Oliver O'Donovan, whom he sees as a fellow Augustinian advocate of secularity.

Through his reappropriation of Martin Luther King Jr's particular form of Augustinian civic liberalism, augmented by an emphasis on virtue and a dialogue with feminism, regulated by a theological dialectic between love and sin, and rejecting secularism while affirming secularity, Gregory hopes to have 'claim[ed] a space for a more dynamic Augustinian civic liberalism that avoids theocracy and status quo defeatism. It puts political existence under religious and moral pressure, but it does not expect salvation from liberal democracy'.[73]

Political theology seems to have arrived at a consensus that the most pessimistic and violent aspects of Hobbes and Machiavelli, the most crass forms of individualism and the most unsophisticated philosophical abstractions associated with modern liberalism must be rejected by Christian theology. However, we are far from consensus on whether liberalism (like modernity) is something we must continue to value and work within, or something beyond which we must urgently move. We are far from consensus on the meaning and value of 'rights', 'justice', 'autonomy' and 'freedom'. And we are perhaps farthest from consensus on what should follow modern liberal democracy. Perhaps the only emerging consensus in this regard is that Jesus Christ and his Church cannot be irrelevant to the conversation.

In the following chapter we will consider the theme of liberation of the oppressed and marginalized in political theology. While this has always been a present theme since the scriptural narration of the Exodus event and the calls of the prophets for peace and justice, it came to the forefront of political theology in new ways in twentieth-century Liberation and 'Contextual' Theologies, theologies which have been critical of some aspects of liberalism but have also been criticized for being too confined by the limits of liberalism and the liberal state.

CHAPTER 7

OPPRESSION, MARGINALIZATION AND LIBERATION

Attention to people who are oppressed and marginalized and to addressing the mechanisms of oppression and marginalization did not appear for the first time in political theology with the rise of Liberation, Black and Feminist Theologies in the twentieth century. What was new in the twentieth century was the opportunity for members of groups which were historically and currently oppressed and marginalized to engage in, write and teach theology in churches and academies. The themes had always been present in political theology from the revelation of YHWH as deliverer of the oppressed and redeemer of the poor in the Exodus event, in the provisions of Torah and in the message of the prophets; to Jesus' self-identification with the prophetic vision, that he had come with good news for the poor, release for the captives and freedom for the oppressed; to the new levels of equality and fraternity across social, ethnic and economic barriers in the first Christian communities. Throughout Christian history, theological themes of liberation have motivated some of the most transformative and influential movements: the rejection of riches for a life of monasticism, the desire to reform abuses of wealth and ownership in the church and movements to end slavery. Although it has not been a central conviction or lived experience of many modern Christians, the majority voice of the Christian tradition has been that there is an integral relationship between spiritual and bodily, religious and social redemption.

In the twentieth century, political theology was brought to a heightened awareness of the needs of the oppressed and marginalized in the church and in society through the work of Liberation and 'Contextual' Theologians. Most Liberation and 'Contextual' Theologians either begin with, or come to discover in the course of their careers, an understanding of the depths of the interrelatedness of various kinds of oppression. While the structures of modern academia and the limits of one person's capacity for activism tend to result in individuals focusing on one aspect of oppression, marginalization and liberation, they are also struck by the futility of battling against one form of oppression without attention to the others. In this chapter we will consider three theologians who each had a clear and particular focus in their work towards liberation who also stressed the interrelation of that focus with other forms of oppression and liberation. Martin Luther King Jr, known globally for his focus on ending racial segregation in the American South, became increasingly concerned in the course of his career for the interrelation between racism, poverty and militarism. Rosemary Radford Ruether, well known as one of the most prominent Feminist Theologians of the twentieth century and whose early work focused on the liberation of Christian theology from the limits of paternalism and androcentrism, also became a pioneer of ecofeminism and the concern for the interrelation of men's exploitation of women and human exploitation of the earth. Finally, we will consider a less well-known theologian, Marcella Althaus-Reid, who was trained in Latin American Liberation Theology and who worked on the interrelation of political, economic and sexual oppression.

MARTIN LUTHER KING JR (1929–68)

The writing of this chapter coincided with the week in which the first national monument to Martin Luther King Jr was opened in Washington, DC. Perhaps it should not be surprising that in a country where over 100 years passed between the abolition of slavery and the illegalization of official segregation we have also seen over 50 years pass between King's death and the opening of the monument. It will be interesting to see whether those who visit the monument come away with any sense of King as theologian. A friend who taught about the Civil Rights Movement in a religion course at a high-ranking American university often told me with lament that his undergraduate students were almost without exception shocked at his suggestion that King and the Civil Rights Movement had anything to do with churches or Christianity. The fact is that although he is perhaps the most globally well-known figure discussed in these pages, few understand King to be one of the most prominent political theologians of the modern era.

Martin Luther King Jr was born the son of a Baptist minister and was himself licensed to preach at the age of 18. He studied sociology and divinity, was ordained in his parents' Baptist church and went on to earn his doctorate in systematic theology. Inspired by the Sermon on the Mount and the non-violent revolution of Gandhi in India, and moved by the inequalities of life and violence committed routinely against African Americans, King became convinced that the time had come for a movement of non-violent direct action for racial equality. Central to his thought and activism was the Gandhian idea that both the oppressed and the oppressor are dehumanized by oppression, so that when the oppressed stands up against the oppressor non-violently, demanding to be treated as a fellow human, this is both an act of asserting one's own dignity and of loving the enemy. Non-violent direct action was meant to shame the enemy by shining a light on their oppression, but the goal of bringing the enemy's oppression to light is not defeat of the enemy, but reconciliation.

King rose to national and global prominence in 1955 and 1956 as he led a boycott of the Montgomery, Alabama public bus system in protest of its racial segregation policies. After a 13-month struggle, the buses were desegregated. This victory was met both with a determination to expand upon it (King founded the Southern Christian Leadership Conference the following year, which would be a central organization in the Civil Rights Movement) and with terror (several shootings, attacks and bombings were carried out against the Montgomery activists in the weeks following the decision to desegregate buses). King became the leader of a movement of non-violent direct action aimed at dismantling the institution of segregation and assuring full and equal rights for African Americans. King was opposed not only by explicitly racist whites who defended segregation and inequality, but by his colleagues and peers on both sides. He was questioned by fellow pastors to his right who told him he was pushing too hard, too soon and too fast. They urged patience and the use of proper, legal channels instead of civil disobedience. To them he wrote the famous 'Letter from a Birmingham Jail' while imprisoned in 1963.[1] He was also questioned by fellow activists and Black Theologians to his left who told him he was being too patient, was conceding too much power to the whites through his message of love and non-violence, and was holding back what was really needed: revolutionary black power. In *Where Do We Go From Here: Chaos or Community?* (1965),[2] he voiced agreement with many of the principles of the Black Power Movement while arguing that violent revolution and black separatism must be rejected.

Though his activist career was only to last 12 years, his agenda was constantly widening and moving forward: from segregation in the South, to national voting rights, to urban poverty in the North, to national economic inequality, to global economic inequality, to the horrors of the Vietnam War. King sparked considerable controversy when he delivered an address to a meeting of the Clergy and Laity Concerned about Vietnam at the Riverside Church in New York City in April of 1967, precisely one year before his assassination. He had been advised and urged to remain focused on civil rights and not be distracted by the anti-war movement, but he had come to a point of being unable to follow such advice. He addressed those who would oppose this move, saying, 'Have they forgotten that my ministry is in obedience to the one who loved his enemies so fully that he died for them? What then can I say to the "Vietcong" or to Castro or to Mao as a faithful minister of this one? Can I threaten them with death or must I not share with them my life?'[3] King believed that his Christianity called him beyond loyalty to the 'causes' of his country, and he urged other Christians to join him in this understanding.

This I believe to be the privilege and the burden of all of us who deem ourselves bound by allegiances and loyalties which are broader and deeper than nationalism and which go beyond our nation's self-defined goals and positions. We are called to speak for the weak, for the voiceless, for victims of our nation and for those it calls enemy, for no document from human hands can make these humans any less our brothers.[4]

In the tragedies and horrors of Vietnam, King saw people being oppressed under the combination of racism, poverty and militarism both at home and abroad. At home, military conscription created a bitter cocktail of racial, economic and militarist injustices.

> [W]e have been repeatedly faced with the cruel irony of watching Negro and white boys on TV screens as they kill and die together for a nation that has been unable to seat them together in the same schools. So we watch them in brutal solidarity burning the huts of a poor village, but we realize that they would never live on the same block in Detroit. I could not be silent in the face of such manipulation of the poor.[5]

And on the ground in Vietnam, it was the poorest of the locals who were suffering the highest price for the war. 'I speak as a child of God and a brother to the suffering poor of Vietnam,' he said. 'I speak for those whose land is being laid waste, whose homes are being destroyed, whose culture is being subverted.'[6]

In this address, King urged the American government to take immediate action to end the war. He specified several steps: stop the bombing, declare a ceasefire, prevent new battlegrounds from opening in neighbouring areas, accept a legitimate role for the National Liberation Front, set a date for withdrawal and make reparations. He also urged sustained action by churches and synagogues, whom he told to keep protesting and to encourage all their young men to be conscientious objectors. More poignantly, he urged people of faith to recognize that the war in Vietnam was 'but a symptom of a far deeper malady within the American spirit' and that if the war was addressed without also addressing this deeper malady, they would only find themselves continuously consumed by protests against other injustices like it. According to King, the deeper malady was the nation's orientation to material and technological gain instead of towards the human person.

> We must rapidly begin the shift from a 'thing-oriented' society to a 'person-oriented' society. When machines and computers, profit motives and property rights are considered more important than people, the giant triplets of racism, materialism and militarism are incapable of being conquered.[7]

King directly challenged the nation's prioritizing of military might over social welfare, saying, 'A nation that continues year after year to spend more money on military defense than on programs of social uplift is approaching spiritual death.'[8]

Feminist and Womanist Theologians would eventually question King and his generation of Black Theologians for their inattention to the oppression of women. King's keen analysis of the interrelation of racial and economic oppression with militarism is striking today both for the courage it takes to speak publicly about this interrelation in America (how many public figures are willing to address this complex of oppression today?) and for its blindness to the realities of gender inequality which are dependent upon as well as roots of these other forms of oppression. We will now consider the work of one feminist who has come to an awareness of another complex of oppression: the relationship between the exploitation of women and the exploitation of the earth.

ROSEMARY RADFORD RUETHER (1936–)

Rosemary Radford Ruether has been one of the most prominent theological feminists since the publication of her first book, *The Church Against Itself*, in 1967. Ruether's theological training was primarily in Patristics. Her early work embodies the concerns of Feminist Theology contemporary with the first generation of political theology, primarily critiquing the sexism and androcentrism of religion and society. In *Religion and Sexism* (1974), she detailed the misogynist aspects of the texts, doctrines and practices of Christianity and Judaism. However, Ruether was also on the leading edge of Feminist Theologians who moved on to constructive Feminist Theology. Her most well-known book, *Sexism and God-Talk* (1983), arose from her lectures on systematic theology from a feminist perspective. She has remained a member of the Catholic Church throughout her life, in contrast to several prominent Feminist Theologians of her generation who felt their theologies necessarily led them out of their churches.

Ruether began her teaching career at a predominantly African-American seminary in Washington, DC during the era of the Civil Rights Movement, and she was actively involved in the movement both in DC and in Mississippi. As the anti-war movement emerged, she also became a prominent peace activist. These movements and her grassroots involvement with the people at the centre of them would profoundly shape her thought. She coined the phrase 'the interstructuring of oppression' in order to highlight the common roots of sexism, racism, classism and degradation of the earth. In addition to her work on sexism, she has written on the subjects of anti-Semitism and political conflict.[9] In particular, Ruether has been a pioneer in ecofeminism. Later in this chapter we will briefly explore her book on the subject, *Gaia and God*. First, we will look at the essay in *Sexism and God-Talk* in which she reflects on various options for feminist political theory, as it offers an important introduction to variations in modern feminisms' interactions with modern social forms and theories.

'The New Earth: Socioeconomic Redemption from Sexism' is the title of Ruether's chapter on feminism and the political in *Sexism and God-Talk*. In it, she claimed that from the beginning of Christianity until the Enlightenment, the equality of all persons inaugurated by Christ was 'understood to apply to a new redeemed order beyond creation, to be realized in Heaven', while the natural order of the creation and the current era continued to be understood hierarchically. Only in and after the Enlightenment was the 'naturalness' of social hierarchy called into question and, according to Ruether, 'The claim that redemption in Christ has a social dimension has come about in modern Christianity only by an identification of its inherited messianic symbols with their secular interpretation in liberalism and socialism'.[10] She then describes how feminism has worked for socio-economic liberation in three different forms: liberalism, socialism and radicalism.

Liberal feminism sought the full inclusion of women in the liberal vision of individual rights. Beginning with the suffrage movement, this vision of feminist socio-economic liberation focused on attaining the same rights for women already held by men (voting, access to higher education, entry into all professions) as well as equality for women when in the same positions as men (in marriage law, property ownership, equality of pay and equal opportunity within all professions). As this movement progressed, it also came to focus on the individual woman's rights to control over her own body. This included activism for rights related to contraception and abortion as well as activism against sexual harassment, domestic violence, rape and pornography. However, the movement eventually came up against the fact that more just laws are not necessarily sufficient for the creation of a more equal society. Even when all the right laws seemed to be in place, liberal feminists continued to observe deep inequalities in society, largely arising from the inequality between post-industrial, paid work outside the home and domestic, unpaid work inside the home. According to Ruether, liberal feminism's inability to overcome this inequality made socialist feminism the next logical progression for many theorists and activists.

'The traditional complaint of socialist feminists against liberal feminism was that its ideology and practice is encapsulated within the class interests of the bourgeois.'[11] In the eyes of socialist feminism, liberal feminists had taken middle-class male roles as the norm and simply worked for middle-class women to have the same rights as middle-class men. 'But they seldom realized the very different concerns of working-class women, racial minority women, and poor women, who were shut out of exercising class-based "rights."'[12] The goal of socialist feminism was economic autonomy for all women. 'Without economic independence under equal working conditions, the civil rights that liberal feminism would win – the rights to vote, to be educated, and to own property – remained class privileges.'[13] Where socialist policies were enacted with gender equality in mind, state programmes made state-paid labour out of tasks otherwise done by unpaid women at home (most commonly childcare but there have also been collectives for other tasks such as laundry, cleaning and cooking). However, at the state level this only slightly lessened work and economic inequality; it did not eliminate it. More radical collectivist experiments had to be smaller in scale, including communes where the private home and nuclear family were abolished in favour of all domestic arrangements being collectivized (communal kitchens, equally shared labour of all types and a dormitory for all the children of the community). Ruether notes the ironic danger of extending this experiment to the state level, namely the surrender of the home to state control: 'In the name of the liberation of women, we would hand over the remnants of that self-employed and autonomous sphere of our life where we own and control our own means of production.'[14] Fundamentally, Ruether argued, socialist feminism offered an important critique of liberal feminism yet failed to move beyond the identification of the normal human life with all things traditionally male. Equality for women in terms of money-earning labour outside the domestic sphere was still the focus. This was the norm from which women were alienated and into which they needed to be integrated. Questioning this assumption, some feminists began to ask, 'Should we not take the creation and sustaining of human life as the center and reintegrate alienated maleness into it?'[15]

From this reorientation arose radical feminism, which focused on the goodness of womanhood and the control of women over their own persons, bodies and lives. This has given rise to several forms of feminist separatism from men and the male, of which Ruether described four: separatist lesbianism in which women chose partnerships with other women in order to exclude men from their primary relationships; spiritual separatism, as in the work of Mary Daly, in which liberation and separation from male oppression is inward and spiritual; Goddess religion which separates from mainstream religion to form goddess-centred beliefs and practices; and feminist work collectives where women work for and with women without male ownership or involvement. Ruether concludes that social arrangements such as lesbian families and women's collectives can only become 'experimental bases for an alternative humanity' if they are not tied to separatist ideology which makes men the enemy. 'Such enemy-making of men would ultimately subvert the whole dream of a women's culture based on mutuality and altruism.'[16] Ruether's own proposal is that feminism needs to incorporate the best aspects of liberalism, socialism and radicalism in seeking a society of equals.

> We seek a society that affirms the values of democratic participation, of the equal value of all persons as the basis for their civil equality and their equal access to the educational and work opportunities of the society. But more, we seek a democratic socialist society that dismantles sexist and class hierarchies, that restores ownership and management of work to the base communities of workers themselves, who then create networks of economic and political relationships. Still more, we seek a society built on organic community, in which the processes of childraising, of education, of work, of culture have been integrated to allow both men and women to share child nurturing and homemaking and also creative activity and decision making in the larger society. Still more, we seek an

ecological society in which human and nonhuman ecological systems have been integrated into harmonious and mutually supportive, rather than antagonistic, relations.[17]

Ruether has no utopian delusions about creating this society. She notes that the work would either involve small, alternative communities where the vision can be realized by like-minded and highly motivated people; or small pieces of the vision being worked on separately and progressively. 'But the alternative non-sexist, non-classist and nonexploitative world eludes us as a global system.'[18]

As most of the chapters in *Sexism and Godtalk* arose from Ruether's lectures in Feminist Theology classes during the 1970s, we can see that from its beginnings Ruether's work showed an awareness of the interrelation of oppression based on sex, class and economics. In the new introduction to the 1993 edition of this work, she noted that she saw no need for fundamental revisions to this early work, but did see the need for further development, particularly on 'the relationship between the domination of women and the domination of nature'. She then described the task of ecofeminism:

> Ecofeminists discern both a symbolic and a structural connection between the mistreatment of women and the mistreatment of nature in patriarchal cultures and social systems. As ancient patriarchal culture shaped its system of female subjugation, it also dethroned the female deities of natural renewal. Patriarchal cultures have seen the bodily world as something both inferior and evil and have imagined a higher, male, spiritual world where this lower world could be both escaped and dominated from outside. Thus, for ecofeminists, the struggle against ecological devastation is interconnected with the struggle against patriarchy.[19]

In *Gaia and God*, Ruether traced the development of deep ecology in parallel to the development of radical feminism as described above. Just as radical feminism 'declared that the issue was deeper' than either liberal or socialist feminism had been aware, and that 'we had to look at the patterns of culture and consciousness that sustain male domination over and violence to women', likewise the development of deep ecology 'took the study of ecology to another level' through its examination of 'the symbolic, psychological, and ethical patterns of destructive relations of humans with nature'.[20] Ecofeminism, then, seeks to combine these two radical and deep studies to 'explore how male domination of women and domination of nature are connected, both in cultural ideology and in social structures'.[21]

While Ruether agrees with deep ecology that Western culture and Christian tradition have 'justified and sacralized these relationships of domination',[22] she also parts company with many ecologists in her conviction that Western culture and Christian theology also contain resources for the healing of human relations to one another and to the earth. Her title, *Gaia and God*, introduces her argument that 'merely replacing a male transcendent deity with an immanent female one' (through the theory of Gaia, named for an earth goddess, which personifies the planet as a living, unified organism), 'is an insufficient answer to the "god-problem"'.[23] Her argument is structured through the concepts of creation, destruction, domination and deceit, and healing. She shows how Christian doctrines of creation, judgement, sin and fallenness, and redemption have both contributed to human domination of nature and also may offer resources for a healing and cooperative relationship. She proposes in particular a focus on the combination of Hebraic and Protestant theological emphases on covenant along with Catholic theological emphases on sacrament. In the tradition of covenant, she finds an understanding of 'intimate unity between justice and right relations to nature in the covenantal relation between God and Israel', especially seen in the biblical legislation on Sabbath and Jubilee, as well as a notion of the church as a covenanted and covenantal community in both Anabaptist and Calvinist traditions. In sacramental theology, she finds a philosophy of nature which unites matter and spirit. She concludes,

> We need both of these holy voices. We cannot depend on volunteerism alone to save rain forests and endangered species, set limits to the exploitation of animals and sanction abusers. We need organized systems and norms of ecological relations. Otherwise, not only will most people not comply, because they have no way of fulfilling their daily needs except through exigencies of the present system. But, without the second voice, our laws have no heart, no roots in compassion and fellow feeling. They fail to foster a motivating desire for biophilic living.[24]

The book concludes with a proposal inspired by Latin American Liberation Theology, the formation of 'base communities of spirituality and resistance'.[25]

MARCELLA ALTHAUS-REID (1952–2009)

Born in Argentina, baptized in the Catholic Church and educated in Latin American Liberation Theology at an ecumenical school of theology in Buenos Aires, Marcella Althaus-Reid first worked in Liberation-Theology-inspired social and community projects in the slums of Buenos Aires. These built on Liberation Theologian, Paulo Freire's work on literacy in impoverished communities. She went on to establish similar literacy programmes in Dundee and Perth, Scotland and to earn a PhD from the University of St Andrews. Her ecclesial journey would take her out of the Catholic Church and into involvement with Quakers, Scottish Presbyterians and the Metropolitan Community Church. Shortly after the completion of her PhD she was appointed to a lectureship at the University of Edinburgh in 1994, where she rose through the academic ranks to become the first woman ever appointed to a chair in their School of Divinity when she was made Professor in 2006. Sadly, her life and career were cut short just three years later when she died of cancer.

Her brief academic career was marked by work on the frontier of Liberation Theology as she sought to bring it into conversation with postcolonialism, gender theory and queer theory.[26] She radicalized the claim of Liberation Theology that theology should begin with, among and from the perspective of the poor by seeking theological insight from socially, economically and sexually marginalized sources such as the graffiti on the cathedral walls and the transvestite nightclubs of Buenos Aires. She called her project 'Indecent Theology', as she explored the social and political expectations and limitations of 'decency' through the Latin American concept of *decencia*. On her personal website, she described the task of Indecent Theology in relation to Latin American Liberation Theology:

> Liberation Theology has helped us to unmask political interests masquerading as 'God's will' in theology. This is called 'ideological suspicion' in theology. To this political suspicion we are adding now a combination of suspicions in the making of

theology: political, economical, racial, colonial and also sexual. The use of these suspicions when we read the Bible or when we reflect on the way that theology tells women what is sin, for instance, and the consequences of that, is a subversive act that I call Indecency. Indecent Theology is a theology which starts with people's lives and critical experiences without censorship.[27]

In one of her last published pieces, Althaus-Reid suggested that Liberation Theology needed a 'counter-guide'. She believed that Liberation Theology had been domesticated in its struggle 'against the market which makes commodities of theological praxis, by replacing creativity and dissent by repetitions without subversion'.[28] Histories of and introductions to Liberation Theology told domesticated accounts. 'I would not start with the episcopal conferences of Meddellín or Puebla,' she wrote. 'Instead, I would start by taking an option for the unprofitable sites of love present in current liberationist praxis, sites of the unproductive, wasteful, gratuitous, rebellious love found at the margins of religious authoritative discourse of power.'[29]

She challenged Liberation Theology by suggesting that its 'hermeneutical circle of theological action and reflection starting from the community of the poor as it is' had been neglectful of the fact that those margins are not only economic and political, and extend even beyond the margins of race and gender: 'those margins are also sexual margins'.[30] She appreciated and embraced Liberation Theology for its 'strategy of dislocation' which 'not only exposed a centre-periphery dynamic of power and constituency in politics, but also denounced that model of dependency in the Church and theology'.[31] According to Althaus-Reid, this 'dislocation' had three important aspects: the dislocation of the subject of theology by making the subject the poor, the dislocation of church organization through the creation of Base Ecclesial Communities and the dislocation of the theologian who is now identified as a situated person with a context and an agenda instead of feigning objectivity and neutrality. Liberation Theology also 'required that Christian dogmas were verified in action, in action related to critical reality'.[32]

However, according to Althaus-Reid, Liberation Theology had failed to see the sexual aspects and implications of its own model of dislocation, praxis and verification. One reason for this oversight is that Liberation Theology had often failed to fulfil its own mandate of starting from the perspective of the poor and marginalized, because it insisted on starting from 'the theologized experiences of the people. By that we mean the experiences of the people after they had been processed through the theological framework of reference of the Church'.[33] Thus, in her project of Indecent Theology, the people's experiences must be the starting point as they are, including their political, economic, racial, gender and sexual aspects, so that theology can function 'at the level of political and social analysis and at the level of thinking about what a theology, which incorporates a sexuality from the margins, can tell us about ourselves and God'.[34]

Since the middle of the twentieth century, each new decade of political theology seems to arrive with a new awareness of a form of oppression and marginalization to which the previous decades' work was insufficiently attentive, and the layers of complex interrelationships between the reasons and the ways in which some dominate and exploit others – the many needs in our world, our societies and our churches which cry out for God's liberation – can become overwhelming. This aspect of political theology leaves some with a sense of zealous determination for transformationist activism. It leaves others with a bitter cynicism about the proliferation of theological –isms and what seems to be an infinite regress in the discovery of the wronged and the blaming of wrongdoers. Second generation political theologians have also noted several theological and methodological issues with first generation, liberationist work. These include an inappropriate dependency upon liberalism in some cases and an insufficiently critical appropriation of Marxism in other cases; an over-reliance on statecraft and state-based solutions; a limitation to the negative aspects of un-masking and deconstructing oppression without sufficient positive, redemptive action (a sense of 'liberation from . . .' without 'liberation for . . .'); and an over-identification with limiting, modernist theory and philosophy. These questions are serious and important. However, they should not drive theologians or students of theology into the mode of bitter cynicism, as if all this business of oppression and liberation was a fad of the twentieth century which has played its part and is no longer needed or welcome. The impulse for socio-political liberation in the scriptures and the Christian tradition has been no fad, and its needfulness never fades.

CHAPTER 8

CREATION, HISTORY AND ESCHATOLOGY

In any field of theological inquiry, it is of utmost importance that our theology is both responsive to the shaping issues of the day, as well as remaining attentive to the shape theology has taken in the Christian tradition. The doctrines of God, Christology, Pneumatology, anthropology, soteriology, ecclesiology and eschatology must always remain on our horizon as the neglect of one or several invariably leads to imbalance in any theological enterprise. Political theology is no different. Thus far we have seen indications of the importance of Christology, anthropology, soteriology and ecclesiology for the shaping of theologies of human politics. Our relation to the ruling Christ and to the life and teachings of Jesus of Nazareth (and our ability to hold these two in unity); our view of human nature, sinfulness and redemption and its consequences for the ordering of our common life; how we relate salvation to the political order (Can the ideal political order 'save' us? Can we 'redeem' social orders?); the relationship between the church and the political as well as the political nature of the church itself – all these have figured prominently in the preceding explorations of historical and contemporary political theology.

Less in evidence thus far in this introduction has been Pneumatology, and I think it is fair to say this is a somewhat neglected doctrine in the field, though there are important exceptions. Jürgen Moltmann's political theology was deeply shaped by his Pneumatology. In *The Church in the Power of the Spirit*, part of his early trilogy along with *Theology of Hope* and *The Crucified God*, Moltmann extended his previous writings on the church as Christologically focused with an eschatological horizon. He explored the work of the Spirit as presence and power, forming the church into an open community of solidarity and transformation. Less well-received by his critics, but more comprehensive in its exploration of Pneumatology was his later work, *The Spirit of Life*.[1]

Mark Lewis Taylor has also noted how the political theologies of North Atlantic theologians of African descent are more attuned to the importance of the Holy Spirit in political theology.[2] Particularly interesting in this regard is the combination of Pentecostalism and Liberation Theology in some of the Black Theology of Britain, especially the work of Robert Beckford. While Black Theology in America has tended to arise from descendants of Africans brought to America in the era of slavery, and from historically black branches of the Baptist or Methodist churches (or other mainline Protestant denominations), Black Theology in Britain has been shaped by post-war migration from the Caribbean to Britain, and the prominence of Pentecostal churches in African Caribbean communities in Britain. In *Dread and Pentecostal: A Political Theology for the Black Church in Britain*, Beckford draws from Rastafarianism and Pentecostalism to develop a holistic liberation theology for black British Christians.[3]

Also relatively unexplored in our Introduction is the doctrine of God and the doctrine of eschatology. In the remainder of this chapter, we will look at the doctrine of creation as an aspect of the doctrine of God, as the interrelation of creation, history and eschatology is one of the most fundamental theological determinants of political theology. We will first consider debates over whether apocalyptic should be opposed in favour of eschatology, or embraced as one aspect or variety of Christian eschatology. We will then briefly explore the relationship between creation and eschatology in Thomas Aquinas.

ESCHATOLOGY AND/OR APOCALYPTIC

Derived from the Greek word for 'last' (*eschatos*), eschatology has often been defined as the doctrine of last things. While some have conceived of the doctrine as describing what will happen at the end of time or the end of human life – particularly the second coming of Christ, death, resurrection, judgement and eternal life – many have conceived of eschatology more broadly in terms of teleology, or ultimate purpose and fulfilment. Christian eschatology asks how God's purposes for humanity and creation will be fulfilled within and in the culmination of earth's history, especially in the second coming of Jesus Christ. Eschatology is not only a doctrine about what will happen at the end, but also about the meaning of Christian life in light of the *eschaton*, or end of history.

Derived from the Greek word *apokalypto* (to reveal), 'apocalyptic' refers to texts or theologies which focus on human beings receiving divine revelations, usually involving a glimpse into a transcendent reality or supernatural world, about future (sometimes cataclysmic and world-ending) events. An 'apocalypse' is an apocalyptic text or the sort of event described in such a text, and 'apocalypticism' refers to social movements or ideologies formed by an apocalyptic perspective. While the books of Isaiah, Zechariah, Ezekiel, Joel and Mark have apocalyptic elements, the fully apocalyptic texts of the Bible are the book of Daniel (particularly chapters 7–12) and the book of Revelation. Throughout Christian history there have been debates about whether or not Revelation truly belongs within the biblical canon. Its mysterious contents and its utter departure in form from all other New Testament texts have left some theologians wondering whether it belongs in the Bible at all. There were many other Jewish and Christian apocalypses written in the intertestamental period and in the first two centuries of Christianity which were not included in the canon. Most apocalypses were likely written during social crises in communities which were somehow alienated from or oppressed by contemporary power holders and structures. Apocalyptic visions often involved the future judgement and/or dismantling of the power structures under which the authors' communities were suffering.

In late-twentieth-century theology, something of a consensus arose that 'apocalypse', 'apocalyptic' and especially 'apocalypticism' connote theological error and ethical danger. According to this view, apocalyptic is the purview of historical and contemporary fanatics. By contrast, *'eschaton'* and 'eschatology' connote theological sophistication and proper ethical normativity; eschatology is the purview of thoughtful Christians who find in it reasonable resources for ethics, including politics. For many theologians, the difference between apocalyptic and eschatology is precisely that the Christian tradition, beginning within the scriptures themselves, has ruled out the normativity of apocalyptic in favour of eschatology. Thus, for many apocalyptic has come to be the opposite of eschatology, instead of one aspect or variety of eschatology within the Jewish and Christian scriptures and traditions. Apocalyptic became identified in particular with millenarian movements, which tend to centre on literalist readings of certain passages of Revelation and usually involve a charismatic leader and a conviction that the second coming and the kingdom of God will be consummated within their lifetime. These movements have been marked by fringe practices ranging from publicizing the date of the second coming to forming cults to violently establishing theocracies.[4]

Such beliefs and practices might well give theologians pause about any positive, normative role for apocalypse in political theology. However, the question is whether problems arise from apocalypse *per se*, or from a particular interpretation of apocalypse. We will explore this question, along with the importance of the interrelationship of creation, history and eschatology, through a consideration of two recent books: Charles Mathewes's *A Theology of Public Life*, and Nathan Kerr's *Christ, History and Apocalyptic*. Both these authors understand themselves to be offering a work of political theology in which a proposal is made for how Christians should live in the world in light of eschatology. And, interestingly, both proposals centre around the ideas – or more accurately, the practices – of doxology and liturgy. However, the two authors take markedly different journeys from the question of Christian ways of life in light of the *eschaton* to proposals centring on doxology and liturgy. Kerr's argument is Yoderian, while Mathewes's is Augustinian. Kerr's proposal is framed in terms of mission, while Mathewes's is framed in terms of citizenship. Kerr's proposal is guided by the metaphor of diaspora, while Mathewes's proposal rejects resident-alien models and seeks a way for Christians to be more embedded and this-worldly. Both seem to focus on particular aspects of apocalyptic: how it holds up the transcendent sovereignty of God and how it signifies a break in the normal relationship between heaven and earth, between human history and the world to come. For Kerr, these are the positive functions of apocalyptic, and an appropriately apocalyptic politics will be orientated both towards the transcendence of God's sovereignty and the 'inbreaking' of that reality in the life, death and resurrection of Jesus Christ in human history. Kerr describes his proposal as 'a vision of history that at once calls for and is empowered by an apocalyptic politics of mission'.[5] This politics of mission turns on the practices of doxology and liturgy. For Kerr, to say that politics should be doxological and that doxology is apocalyptic is to say that 'the quintessence of Christian political action is to be located at the point where God's activity interrupts all forms of politic *givenness* through the enactment of Jesus' apocalyptic historicity.'[6]

For Mathewes, these aspects of apocalyptic are precisely what make it an unfaithful political orientation, as he identifies them with looking for ways out of the here and now, and identifying God and Christianity with movement away from the world and history. Thus he explicitly rejects apocalyptic, calling his proposal eschatological and anti-apocalyptic. Mathewes describes his project as a theology and an ascetics (a teaching or discipline) of 'faithful Christian citizenship' which will 'promote Christians' engagement in public life during the world and inform their understanding of the shape and purpose of such life', as well as 'training them in their fundamental vocation as citizens of the kingdom of heaven, particularly considering those forces that mis-shape our engagement in public life today'.[7]

For Kerr, Christian apocalyptic is 'a mode of taking seriously the intrinsically political character of the church's mission'.[8] Kerr argues that 'the inbreaking of God's reign – the apocalyptic politics of Jesus – is made real and available as a way of seeing or an imaginative act (doxology) and as a mode of work (liturgy) that concur as that praxis by which the world (and thereby also the church) is converted by and to the subversive excess of God's coming Kingdom'.[9] Using the theme of diaspora from the work of Yoder, Kerr concludes that 'diasporic existence occurs as a very particular kind of exile from the given power structures of the world in solidarity with those marginalized and oppressed by those powers'.[10]

According to Mathewes, Augustine was 'the first major figure to use eschatology to resist a too literal apocalypticism'.[11] Mathewes describes apocalyptic as dangerous for two reasons. First, it seeks epistemological closure, a sure knowledge of what will happen and when and how. Second, it is escapist and other-worldly; it longs for dramatic escape from this evil world. Instead, Mathewes wants to propose that Christians should live 'eschatologically . . . during the world'.[12] The world, in this sense, is more 'an era than a place', and Christians are 'other-temporalitied', not otherworldly.[13] In other words, Christian life in history should be conditioned by the horizon of the coming new era instead of by an idea that Christian citizenship is in another place. Mathewes argues that the world itself is 'a form of participation, through Christ, in the church, in the divine perichoresis', the inter-penetrating common life of the Triune God.[14] Citizenship during the world is 'liturgical' in that it is 'an activity that the body of Christ undertakes in doxological praise of God as Creator, Sustainer, and Redeemer', which means that 'civic life can be performed in a way that is continuous with the liturgy of the blessed in heaven that is our eschatological destiny'.[15]

We can see why some aspects of political theologies such as Kerr's might make Mathewes nervous. Mathewes very helpfully insists that 'Creation is not the "background" to our redemption, it plays an essential role within it',[16] whereas creation seems almost entirely absent from Kerr's argument. While Kerr is critical of Hauerwasian views of church-as-polis, he nonetheless makes his constructive argument in stark terms of 'church' and 'world' in a way which seems deeply connected to anthropology, soteriology and ecclesiology, while neglectful of Theology proper and of the doctrine of creation in particular. And while Mathewes calls for a properly Christian this-worldliness, arguing that we can in fact meet God in the world, Kerr consistently speaks of the work of God in relation to the world in dualistic, almost violent terms of inbreaking, rupture and interruption.

However, we can also see why political theologies such as Mathewes's would frustrate someone like Kerr. Kerr very helpfully focuses on apocalyptic as opening new ways of seeing. It is not clear why Mathewes needs to hold to a particular definition of apocalyptic as foreclosing instead of opening, a definition which supports the theological consensus that eschatology is good and apocalyptic is bad. He does not seem willing to find what is constructive for political theology in the apocalyptic elements of scripture and the Christian tradition.

One of the reasons why apocalyptic has fallen afoul of theological consensus is the equation of apocalypse with a cataclysmic event which ends the world and its history. Critics of apocalyptic are correct to resist the desire for a new world at the cost of destruction of this world, and longing for the future at the cost of eclipsing the significance of history. However, if apocalypse is reframed in the senses of the Greek, *apokalypsis*, of unveiling, revelation and disclosure, instead of as world-ending cataclysm, what might be the potential ramifications for political theology? Perhaps through apocalypse-as-unveiling, we can capture the best of what people like Mathewes and Kerr are saying without falling into the potential ditches on either side of them. We can seek a political theology which is grounded in the goodness and God-intendedness of creation while also remaining open to new ways of perceiving history, politics and the future through the apocalyptic.

If cataclysm is not central to apocalyptic, instead of being a revelation of the coming cataclysmic destruction of the world, apocalyptic becomes an unveiling of deep truths about the world and the social order which requires dramatic rhetoric for the deconstruction of the status quo and of claims to power and ultimacy. When apocalypse moves from cataclysm to unveiling, from destruction to deconstruction, it becomes clear how we can argue that Christian apocalyptic can be deeply and normatively doxological, as in Kerr. Kerr's use of Yoder mainly focuses on *The Politics of Jesus*, but in a lesser-known essay derived from an address Yoder gave during the 1980s nuclear arms race, Yoder made precisely this argument about apocalyptic.[17] Drawing on a quotation from Larry Rasmussen, Yoder described apocalyptic as a vehicle through which the believing community can '"deconstruct" the self-evident picture of how things are which those in power use to explain that they cannot but stay that way'.[18] He noted that the sort of communities from which biblical apocalyptic texts arose needed 'first of all to know not what they would do if they were rulers, nor how to seize power, but that the present power constellation which oppresses them is not the last word'.[19] Yoder cited as an example the first vision of John in

Revelation, the vision of all the heavenly hosts worshipping the lamb that was slain, and he called the hymnody reflected there 'performative proclamation' which 'redefines the cosmos in a way prerequisite to the moral independence which it takes to speak truth to power'.[20] Mathewes's concern regarding the epistemological closure of apocalyptic is answered here. He suggests that apocalyptic gives people an undue confidence and sense of finality in their knowledge through its claim to reveal the future. However, apocalyptic only creates such epistemological closure when apocalyptic texts are read literally as predictions of future events. If apocalyptic is not a revelation of specific future events but an imaginative vision of the future which functions to jolt us out of our status-quo perceptions and see current social reality for what it truly is in relation to God, our ways of knowing are newly opened, not dangerously closed.

Having orientated our attention to apocalyptic away from cataclysm and destruction, we can be reorientated to the ways in which apocalyptic also offers visions of the ultimate healing and renewal of all creation. In Revelation, for example, we see not the utter destruction and abandonment of creation, but its renewal: a new heaven and a new earth. Rowan Williams has suggested that in the time between Jesus' ascension and his return, 'the things and persons of this world are seen in a new way, seen as charged with hope, with a future of glory and of healing. They are seen as if already part of the new heaven and new earth in which God's purposes have been brought to completion'.[21] He goes on to say that Jesus' physical departure from earth 'does not mean that he has abandoned the world, so that we must go and look for him outside it – "looking up into the sky" like the disciples. His life is being lived in us: the new world is being brought to birth in us, gradually and sometimes painfully. We are caught up in the eternal movement of God's commitment to his creation'.[22] This answers Mathewes's concern about escapism. Apocalypticism is indeed escapist if it trades in ideas like rapture, the idea that true believers will be taken up into the clouds with Jesus before the cataclysmic events of the 'great tribulation' begin. However, this is not the case if apocalyptic is not a revelation of a cataclysm or an evil world from which we need to escape. Rather it is an unveiling of realities behind and beyond the current status quo, and one of those realities is the future healing and glorification of creation into which we are being caught up with God.

Christian apocalyptic can be ethically and politically normative when apocalypse is reclaimed as an unveiling of ultimate reality which involves both the deconstruction of contemporary social and political realities, as well as the constructive revelation of a vision of a positive future of the healing of creation. Properly Christian apocalyptic questions standard accounts and opens the possibility of seeing reality differently. The reader or audience of authentic apocalyptic discourse becomes aware that social and political realities are not as they seem, and oppressive claims to power and ultimacy collapse before visions of the sovereignty of God. Through apocalyptic, the believing community also makes and receives proclamations that the God who is in control of human history ultimately seeks the healing and flourishing of all creation.

What I am actually suggesting is that a Yoderian understanding of the political significance of apocalyptic is well-served by being put into conversation with an understanding of creation and eschatology derived from Aquinas, so it is to this aspect of Thomas that we now will turn.

CREATION AND ESCHATOLOGY IN AQUINAS

When 'Augustine' and 'political theology' are said in the same sentence, references to Book XIX of *City of God* are almost sure to follow. Likewise, when 'Aquinas' and 'political theology' are said in the same sentence, references to his discussion of natural law in the *Summa Theologiae* are almost sure to follow. As we saw in Chapter 2, focus on natural law apart from scripture and theology cannot adequately represent or employ Thomas's thought. Likewise, limiting ourselves merely to the observation that there are aspects of government and law which are considered 'natural' by Thomas is to miss some of the most important resources in his thought for political theology. I will briefly consider several aspects of his thought which can provide a needed framework of creation and eschatology for the perspective on human history needed to form faithful political theologies.

Aquinas is at the heart of the tradition which emphasizes the doctrine of *creatio ex nihilo*, creation out of nothing. The conviction that God created all that is out of nothing affirms that creation is God's free gift. God created in utter freedom with no pre-existing cause or necessity and no pre-existing material. All that exists, exists in and from God's free giving of existence. According to Aquinas, the giving of this gift was not an historical event, but is the reality within which history occurs. Creation in Aquinas is not only about an act which brought about the beginning of all that is. All that exists, exists from, in and towards God. It is the constant, loving life of God which allows for the existence of creation. Thus, when we speak of creation we are not speaking only of genesis, of origin, but of the nature of the relation between Creator and creatures, between God who exists without cause and all else which is dependent upon God for existence.

The Creator God is the ever-present source and goal of all creation. Thus, when Thomas takes up the notion of 'common good' from Aristotle, he does not employ it in Aristotle's limited sense; rather, he reads Aristotle through Christian theology which identifies God as the only one who is truly Good and the source of all human good. Thus the common good becomes tied up in our creation and our end in God. Through the ordering of common life towards the good, our sociality becomes participation in the goodness of God. However, this participation is only partial now, as we will only fully participate in the divine goodness in the fullness of the kingdom of God. For Aquinas, creation and eschatology are inextricably related. Eschatology is about God bringing to completion the work and the goal of creation. The world will be taken up into God's glory, and it is towards this glorification and perfect union with God, or beatitude, that we orientate and order our lives, personal and political, in human history. Our forerunner is Jesus Christ, whose resurrection revealed the glorification of a human being within history.

In this brief sketch,[23] we can see how creation, the 'natural', the common good and eschatology are all interrelated in Thomas. In relation to political theology, 'The *telos* or end of the common good is the ordering of right relations between the created order and God as Maker and Ruler of all. The created order is what Thomas calls "nature" and governance is an art that should *imitate* nature as much as possible'.[24] The potential pitfalls of Thomistic political theology are apparent here as well. Critics of Aquinas, especially some feminists, have deemed his political theology unusable because of how it can be employed to equate oppression and injustice with the natural order. This is not surprising as Thomas himself repeatedly affirmed subordination and subjection of women to men as part of the created order. For Aquinas, the relationship of woman to man was analogous to the relation of humans to God. This is indeed an unusable part of his thought which we cannot ignore. We can, however, see that it is not a *necessary* aspect of his theology, as has been argued by several feminists who find in Aquinas most promising resources for Feminist Theology, ethics and politics.[25] Nor can we ignore the long history of 'Thomisms' which employ Aquinas to defend injustice, oppression and violence. In Mark Jordan's provocative work, *Rewritten Theology*, he argues that such uses of Thomas result from a rewriting of Thomism which excises aspects of Thomas's own moral teaching. Jordan's argument, however, is not meant to gloss over what is most difficult in Thomas or in his interpreters. In the chapter titled 'St Thomas and the Police', he uses 'police' to refer to the varieties of foreclosing, oppressive and even violent authoritarianisms which have gone under the name of 'Thomism':

> Sharp questions about Thomas. We cannot duck them or dismiss them. We cannot resolve them with happily ingenious answers. We have to hear them – and in their sharpest form. The question is not, could Thomas have written better? (Yes, probably, but he wrote well enough to require the police to rewrite him.) Nor is the question, do Thomas's texts contain something that attracts the police? (Yes, necessarily, because he is trying to write persuasively about the claims of divinity on human lives.) The sharpest question is, have so many betrayals been fused into Thomas's texts that the only readers willing to persist with them are the police? I want to answer, 'no,' but I see that the answer cannot be given once and for all, because it must be given in the presence of the police – and their victims.[26]

The seriousness with which Aquinas views human sin and limitation has been obscured by the combination of two aspects of his 'rewriting': the way his comments on natural law have been excised and read apart from their theological context, and the overstatement of his supposed optimism in human nature as contrasted with Augustine's pessimism. Here we do well to remember Thomas's basic affinity with Augustine, which includes an emphasis on the gravity and significance of original sin. For Aquinas, neither the loving goodness of God nor the basic inclination of nature towards the good cancels human free will. Thus, an important corrective to forms of Thomism which identify oppressive social orders as natural is the reminder of Aquinas's focus on humans as rational makers of choice. This is not to be confused with the rationalism or the autonomous choosing self of modernity. It is rather again Thomas taking Aristotle up into the Christian tradition; it is the practical rationality of the classical tradition read theologically. Human choices respond to God's free gift of creation, either in gratitude which chooses to follow nature's inclination towards the good and cultivate the virtues and practices which draw us nearer to the Good, or in ingratitude which follows sinful inclinations and disregards the virtues and the common good. Thus, the common good (like the good of each person) is a complex combination of natural inclination and chosen responses.

The consequence of this complexity is the necessity of understanding that political theology formed by this tradition must also be always carefully discerning of this combination so as not to identify sinful human choices and their consequences with what is natural, with created intent or with the good. With this crucial proviso, Aquinas's interrelation of creation, history, eschatology and the ordering of societies towards the common good offers an important theological frame for political theology, and one which has been at the heart of both Catholic Social Teaching and Liberation Theology.

CONCLUSION

By way of conclusion to this introduction to political theology, I would like not only to summarize the ground we have covered in the previous chapters, but also to reconsider the content in relation to the unity of the parts. Each of the previous chapters could with profit be read on its own as an introduction to a specific aspect or issue of political theology, but I would like to reframe them here in relation to an interdependent and interrelated whole.

In Part One we began to see something of the complexity of various meanings, beginnings and understandings of political theology, and we began to see ways of clarifying these complexities through relating the work of various political theologians to specific trajectories, approaches, traditions and schools of thought. Political theology emerged as an important aspect of Christian thought in at least three moments. First and foremost is the political theology of the Bible. The narratives and theology of scripture are permeated throughout with political themes and significance: the relationship between YHWH and Israel, between Israel and her kings and between Israel and nations and empires, including where the people were held in captivity; the sociopolitical aspects of the warnings and admonitions given by the Hebrew prophets; the pervasive importance of the kingdom of God and God's sovereign rule; the incarnation, ministry, teachings, death and resurrection of Jesus Christ; the formation of the church and her relation to the Roman Empire; and the in-between nature of the church's life after the ascension of Christ to rule at the Father's right hand but before his return in glory.

The pervasive presence of the political in scripture did not escape the notice of the church's early theologians. It is the thought of St Augustine in particular, and especially his seminal work, *City of God*, which described the political significance of Christianity in such a persuasive and provocative way that theologians have returned to it again and again throughout Christian history as a catalyst, source or foil for their own political theology. His work is often considered to signal the emergence of political theology outside the scriptures.

And although theologians from St Augustine's time forward have continued the task of relating Christian theology to the political in general as well as to the particular political arrangements and issues of their day, it was in the twentieth century that political theology first came to be understood and labelled as a distinct discipline. As the pluralism of Western societies increased while the likelihood of the inevitability of secularization decreased, and as the official authorities and gatherings of the Christian churches grappled with their relationship to modernity, a moment arose in which many recognized the need for a renewal of political theology. From German Christians struggling with the legacy of the Holocaust and their churches' complicity in the Third Reich; to Latin American Christians struggling with their churches' complicity in economic injustice and corrupt, militant regimes; to black and female Christians in North America struggling with their churches' complicity in racism and sexism; to other Christians in North America struggling with their churches' inability to find language or action which could create and sustain public moral consensus – theologians across the Western world were awoken to the need of the church and the academy to revisit and reinterpret the relationship between the theological and the political. Twentieth-century political theology would emerge in three related but distinct forms, with Political Theology arising in Germany, Liberation Theology arising in Latin America accompanied by Black and Feminist Theologies in North America and Public Theology also arising in North America.

In the late twentieth century and early twenty-first century it began to be clear that a second generation was following these original schools of thought in ways which both built upon them and offered significant critiques of them. Instead of seeking movement from particularly Christian convictions towards more 'universal' or 'public' language or action, these theologians have tended to focus on the particularly Christian as truly universal and public. Instead of struggling with the issues surrounding secularization, these theologians have tended to question whether the 'secular' is a myth. Instead of being happy to work as critical friends within modernity and its characteristic forms of liberalism and democracy, these theologians have tended to offer more direct critiques of modernity, liberalism and liberal democracy. Instead of focusing on the state or the individual within the state as the primary concern of political theology, these theologians have tended to focus on the church. In its more Barthian and scripturally focused form of Postliberal Theology, or its more Catholic and philosophically attuned form of Radical Orthodoxy, or its 'contextual' forms such as Queer Theology, the second generation continues to emerge as a body of work which values liturgy over statecraft.

However, alignment with one of the first or second generation schools of thought does not tell us all we need to know in order to understand variations in political theologies, nor can it illuminate political theology before the twentieth century. Two other central variables are most formative of and helpful in identifying and understanding differing approaches to political theology. The first is often called 'optimism' versus 'pessimism'. This may be understood in relation to alignment with either Augustinian or Thomistic understandings of government in relation to creation and fall as well as theological anthropology; or it may be in relation to understanding government either in terms of Hobbesian contract or Reformed understandings of covenant; or it may be whether one identifies government more with the goodness of creation or the corruption of the 'principalities and powers'. The other, related variable is the theological and ecclesial tradition within which political theology is done, or from which it emerges. The Lutheran, Reformed, Anabaptist, Anglican, Roman Catholic and Orthodox churches and theological traditions each have distinctive formative influences, emphases and histories.

Having thus broken down political theology into trajectories, movements and schools of thought – a crucial exercise for finding one's way into this complex discipline – it is now equally important to recast various components as parts of a theological whole. Part Two of this book began and ended with two of the most fundamental sets of questions and themes in political theology. We began in Chapter 3 with the question which has remained at the centre of political theology throughout Christian history: what is the relationship between the church and the political authorities and arrangements of human societies? We saw how this question has taken on different forms in different eras of Christianity, as well as within the lives and work of Martin Luther during the sixteenth-century Reformation and Karl Barth and Dietrich Bonhoeffer during the

Third Reich and World War II. We ended Part Two in Chapter 8 with the themes which frame all of political theology: creation, history and eschatology. Through the theology of St Thomas Aquinas as well as an exploration of the distinction between eschatology and apocalyptic, we saw how understandings of what human beings and human societies are created for, and the ends towards which they are moving and orientated shape our understandings of the significance of the ordering of human sociality during the history which lies within and between creation and the *eschaton*.

It is most helpful to understand the topics of Chapters 4 through to 7 not as free-standing issues in a list of things which have interested some political theologians, but rather as some of the most prominent themes which radiate from the central issue of the church and the political while being framed by understandings of Christians' role within history as citizens of the coming kingdom, created by God and destined with all creation for God's glory. Chapter 4's exploration of the politics of Jesus asked whether the teachings and example of Jesus might be the best guide to understanding our role within history, and if so, how the politics of Jesus can be lived today. We saw how the normativity of Jesus has been at the heart of Anabaptist political theologies and how this has taken different shapes in sixteenth-century Anabaptism and in the twentieth-century work of John Howard Yoder and his rebuttals of Reinhold Niebuhr.

Chapter 5 explored the implications of the role of Christianity within history for the question of violence. Must Christians sometimes resort to the use of violence in order to be responsible within history, or must Christians be those who resolutely reject violence as a means to fulfilling the peaceful purposes in and for which we were created? Is the church ordained to be an instrument of peace, living in the already of the kingdom, while the state is ordained to be an instrument of violence within the realities of the not yet? How do we respond to the nearly opposite theory that secular states are the protectors of peace while religion is particularly prone to cause violence? We explored some of the roots of these questions in the complexity of St Augustine's theologies of violence and peace. We also looked at some recent manifestations of these questions in Jean Bethke Elshtain's defence of the War on Terror and William Cavanaugh's critique of the idea of religious violence.

In Chapter 6 we considered theological responses to a particular form of social order, modern liberalism and explored why many second generation political theologians, including Stanley Hauerwas and John Milbank, consider it an insufficient model for the ordering of common life within human history – one which is dependent upon an insufficient model of the relationship between the church and the political. Other reasons for widespread criticism of liberalism include questions about its account of creation (the 'natural' state of human competitive self-interest) as well as eschatology (with its rejection of the teleological horizon offered by Christian theology and its replacement by the bastardized eschatology of history as a story of consistent human progress).

Finally, in Chapter 7 we explored liberation as a theme of God's purposes and the church's role in history. Confidence in the equality of human beings as created by God as well as in our mutual ultimate destiny in God has compelled theological attention to wide varieties of marginalization and oppression and their interrelatedness, as well as theological resources for liberation. We saw how Martin Luther King Jr's quest for racial liberation drew his attention to the interrelation of racial oppression with poverty and militarism; how Rosemary Radford Ruether's quest for the liberation of women led her to the interrelation of sexism and the exploitation of the earth; and how the work of Marcella Althaus-Reid was attentive to the interrelation of political, economic and sexual marginalization.

It is my hope that recasting the work of the previous chapters in this way not only aids readers in their comprehension of the coherence of the field, but that it will go some way towards fulfilling the wider intention of this book as stated in the Introduction. It is my hope that the combination of the map of the terrain offered in Part One along with the tasting sessions offered in Part Two, the road signs to the next level of exploration offered in the endnotes and the reframing of these parts in relation to the whole offered in this Conclusion will give readers the tools and confidence needed not only to read further and understand more clearly, but to engage the intersection of theology and politics in their own lives and communities more thoughtfully and intentionally. For all their varieties in sources, approaches and conclusions, what is most fundamentally shared in common by all the biblical authors and the authors of political theology we have discussed is that political theology was the catalyst for, and reflection upon, lived reality and active practice; it has never been intended as an exercise in pure theory.

NOTES

INTRODUCTION

1 Richard Dawkins, *A Devil's Chaplain: Reflections on Hope, Lies, Science, and Love* (London: Weidenfeld and Nicolson, 2003), 157.

2 Mark Juergensmeyer, *Terror in the Mind of God: The Global Rise of Religious Violence* (Berkeley: University of California Press, 2003), 15.

3 Peter Scott and William T. Cavanaugh, eds. *The Blackwell Companion to Political Theology* (Oxford: Blackwell, 2004), 2.

4 The decision to cover only Christian political theology in this volume arises from two unavoidable realities: political theologies of other faiths could not adequately be covered in addition within a volume of this length and scope, and the author is herself a Christian theologian. On Islam, see Bustami Mohamed Khir, 'The Islamic Quest for Sociopolitical Justice', in *The Blackwell Companion to Political Theology*, 503–18; and Antony Black, *The History of Islamic Political Thought* (Edinburgh: Edinburgh University Press, 2001). On Judaism see Peter Ochs, 'Abrahamic Theo-politics: A Jewish View', in *The Blackwell Companion to Political Theology*, 519–34; and David Novak, *Covenantal Rights: A Study in Jewish Political Theory* (Princeton: Princeton University Press, 2000).

5 See St Augustine, *City of God*, trans. Henry Bettenson (London: Penguin Books, 1972), especially Book VI. All citations below are taken from this translation.

6 Carl Schmitt, *Political Theology: Four Chapters on the Concept of Sovereignty* (Chicago: University of Chicago Press, 1985), 36.

7 William T. Cavanaugh, *Migrations of the Holy: God, State, and the Political Meaning of the Church* (Grand Rapids: Eerdmans, 2011).

8 For example, see Michael Hollerich, 'Carl Schmitt', in *The Blackwell Companion to Political Theology*, 116–17.

9 Creston Davis, 'Political Theology – The Continental Shift', *Political Theology* 11.1 (2010): 7–8.

10 D. Stephen Long, 'What Makes Theology "Political"? "Come Let us Reason Together"', *Political Theology* 5:4 (2004): 393–409.

11 See Robert N. Bellah and Steven M. Tipton, eds, *The Robert Bellah Reader* (Durham, NC: Duke University Press, 2006).

CHAPTER 1

1 Walter Brueggemann, 'Scripture: Old Testament', in *The Blackwell Companion to Political Theology*, 9.

2 Ibid., 18.

3 Christopher Rowland, 'Scripture: New Testament', in *The Blackwell Companion to Political Theology*, 32.

4 Less evident in this overview will be in-depth treatment of political theology in the Pauline literature, but this is not neglected by Yoder or O'Donovan, nor by political theologians in general. Indeed, there has been a recent renewal of interest in Paul and political theology, especially among Continental philosophers. See John Milbank, Slavoj Žižek and Creston Davis, *Paul's New Moment: Continental Philosophy and the Future of Christian Theology* (Grand Rapids: Brazos Press, 2010).

5 John Howard Yoder, *The Politics of Jesus* (Grand Rapids: Eerdmans 1972, and 2nd edn, 1994).

6 In addition to *The Politics of Jesus*, Yoder's works of political theology include *The Christian Witness to the State* (Faith & Life Press, 1964 and Scottdale, PA: Herald Press, 2002), *The Priestly Kingdom* (Notre Dame: Notre Dame University Press, 1984) and *For the Nations: Essays Public and Evangelical* (Grand Rapids: Eerdmans, 1997).

7 See Yoder, *The Jewish-Christian Schism Revisited* (London: SCM Press, 2003).

8 Yoder, 'See How They Go with Their Face to the Sun', in *For the Nations*, 60.

9 Ibid., 53.

10 Ibid., 69.

11 Yoder, *Preface to Theology: Christology and Theological Method* (Grand Rapids: Brazos Press, 2002), 243ff. See also 'To Serve Our God

and to Rule the World', in *The Royal Priesthood: Essays Ecclesiological and Ecumenical* (Grand Rapids: Eerdmans, 1994), 133f.

12 Yoder, *The Politics of Jesus*, 38–9.

13 See Yoder, 'Peace without Eschatology?', in *The Royal Priesthood*, 146–7.

14 Yoder, 'Christ the Light of the World', in *The Royal Priesthood*, 185.

15 Yoder, 'Peace without Eschatology?', 147.

16 Yoder, *The Politics of Jesus*, 232. See also 'Christ the Hope of the World', in *The Royal Priesthood*, 218; and *Preface to Theology*, 247–8.

17 Yoder, *The Politics of Jesus*, 246.

18 Yoder, 'Peace without Eschatology?', 151.

19 See Yoder, *The Politics of Jesus*, 231ff.; 'To Serve Our God and to Rule the World', 128 ff.; 'Peace without Eschatology?', 151; 'The Spirit of God and the Politics of Men', in *For the Nations*, 235.

20 See Yoder, *Preface to Theology*, 248. See also 'Peace without Eschatology?', 151.

21 Yoder, *Preface to Theology*, 247–8.

22 Yoder, 'The Otherness of the Church', in *The Royal Priesthood*, 61. See also *The Christian Witness to the State*, 13; and 'Peace without Eschatology?', 151, 163.

23 Yoder, *The Christian Witness to the State*, 10–11.

24 Yoder expands upon this in *The Christian Witness to the State*.

25 Yoder, *Preface to Theology*, 248.

26 Yoder, 'Are You the One Who Is to Come?', in *For the Nations*, 216.

27 Yoder, *Christian Witness to the State*, 10.

28 See especially 'The Constantinian Sources of Christian Social Ethics', and 'The Otherness of the Church'.

29 Yoder, 'The Constantinian Sources of Christian Social Ethics', 135.

30 Ibid., 136.

31 Yoder criticizes 'chaplaincy' in many places. This is not necessarily a critique of all professions which we now refer to as chaplaincy, rather it is a critique of churches' and individuals' willingness to 'presuppose the adequacy and legitimacy of the structures' of societies and institutions in ways which limit their role to blessing and baptizing the status quo while being unable to question or speak prophetically. See *For the Nations*, 119–20.

32 This is expanded upon in 'The Constantinian Sources of Christian Social Ethics'.

33 Yoder, *The Politics of Jesus*, 201.

34 Yoder, *The Christian Witness to the State*, 75–6.

35 Ibid., 77.

36 Yoder, *The Politics of Jesus*, 198.

37 Luke Bretherton, 'Introduction: Oliver O'Donovan's Political Theology and the Liberal Imperative', *Political Theology* 9.3 (2008): 268.

38 Ibid. O'Donovan's works in political theology include *The Desire of the Nations: Rediscovering the Roots of Political Theology* (Cambridge: Cambridge University Press, 1996), *The Ways of Judgment* (Grand Rapids: Eerdmans, 2005), *The Just War Revisited* (Cambridge: Cambridge University Press, 2003) and (with Joan Lockwood O'Donovan) *Bonds of Imperfection: Christian Politics, Past and Present* (Grand Rapids: Eerdmans, 2004).

39 O'Donovan, *The Desire of the Nations*, 27.

40 Ibid., 28.

41 Ibid., 61.

42 Ibid., 83.

43 Ibid., 117.

44 Ibid., 116.

45 Ibid., 117.

46 Ibid., 93.

47 Ibid., 146.

48 Ibid., 121–2.

49 Ibid., 152.

50 Ibid., 151.

51 Ibid., 153.

52 Ibid., 159 and 162.

53 Ibid., 166.

54 Ibid., 195.

55 Ibid., 194.

56 Ibid., 230.

57 See page 52 below.

58 O'Donnovan, *The Desire of the Nations*, 217.

59 Rowan Williams, 'Politics and the Soul: A Reading of the *City of God*', *Milltown Studies* 19/20 (Spring and Autumn 1987): 57, 58.

60 St Augustine, *City of God*, Book XIV, chapter 28.

61 Ibid., Book XVIII, chapter 54.

62 Unfortunately, this point is entirely missed by Yoder, who often aims his criticisms of the Constantinian shift at Augustine. See for examples, 'The Constantinian Sources of Western Social Ethics', 136; 'Peace without Eschatology?', 154; and 'The Otherness of the Church', 157. A much more appropriate target for his critique would perhaps have been Eusebius, who did in fact identify the empire with the kingdom of God. A more careful and sympathetic reading of *City of God* reveals that Augustine's concepts of the two cities are largely compatible with Yoder's understanding of two realms – one in which Christ's sovereignty over all the earth is recognized though not yet fully realized, and another in which it is denied – as in *The Christian Witness to the State*.

63 Augustine as proponent of a 'secular' sphere has been most famously argued for by Robert Markus in a work which was the benchmark of Augustine scholarship for decades, but which has now been widely contested, especially by Rowan Williams, John Milbank, Oliver O'Donovan and William Cavanaugh. R. A. Markus, *Saeculum: History and Society in the Theology of St Augustine* (Cambridge: Cambridge University Press, 1970).

64 William Cavanaugh, 'From One City to Two: Christian Reimagining of Political Space', in *Migrations of the Holy: God, State, and the Political Meaning of the Church* (Grand Rapids: Eerdmans, 2011), 56.

65 Ibid., 57–8.

66 For a brief and interesting introduction to discussions of the secularization thesis and its demise, see Peter Berger, Grace Davie and Effie Fokas, *Religious America, Secular Europe? A Theme and Variation* (Aldershot: Ashgate, 2008).

CHAPTER 2

1 Walter Wink, *Engaging the Powers: Discernment and Resistance in a World of Domination* (Minneapolis: Fortress Press, 1992).

2 R. W. Dyson, 'Introduction', in *St Thomas Aquinas: Political Writings* (Cambridge: Cambridge University Press, 2002), xxiv–xxvi. All quotations of Aquinas below are from Dyson's translation.

3 As with all premodern theologians, it is problematic to tease apart the writings of Aquinas, identifying some as 'theological', others as 'philosophical' and still others as 'political'. However, insofar as his political theology can be isolated, it is generally thought to be most represented in his treatise *De regimine principum,* and in the sections of the *Summa Theologiae*, Ia. 96 and IaIIae. The key sections are gathered in one volume by Dyson.

4 Thomas Aquinas, *De regimine principum*, Book 1, chapter V.

5 Aquinas, *De regimine principum*, Book 1, chapter II.

6 Ibid., Book 1, chapter XV.

7 Aristotle, *The Politics,* trans. Ernst Barker (Oxford: Oxford University Press, 1995), Book 1, Section 1253a.

8 Aquinas, *De regimine principum*, Book 1, chapter 1.

9 Frederick Christian Bauerschmidt, 'Aquinas', in *The Blackwell Companion to Political Theology*, 56.

10 For two contemporary works on natural law approaching these issues in very different ways, see a secularized approach in John Finnis, *Natural Law and Natural Rights*, 2nd edn (New York: Oxford University Press, 2011); and a theological approach in Jean Porter, *Natural Law and Divine Law: Reclaiming the Tradition for Christian Ethics* (Grand Rapids: Eerdmans, 1999).

11 See especially Aquinas, *Summa Theologiae*, IaIIae. 90–7.

12 Ibid., IaIIae. 91. 2. *responsio.*

13 Augustine, *City of God*, Book XIX, chapter 15.

14 Aquinas, *Summa Theologiae*, Ia. 96. 4. *responsio.*

15 Jürgen Moltmann, 'Covenant or Leviathan? Political Theology for Modern Times', *Scottish Journal of Theology* 47 (1994): 19–41.

16 Thomas Hobbes, *Leviathan: Revised Student Edition*, ed. Richard Tuck (Cambridge: Cambridge University Press, 1996).

17 John Milbank, *Theology and Social Theory: Beyond Secular Reason* (Oxford: Blackwell Publishing, 1990).

18 Moltmann, 'Covenant or Leviathan?', 35 and 37.

19 Michael Kirwan, *Political Theology: A New Introduction* (London: Darton, Longman & Todd, 2008), 16–33.

20 For an introduction to Catholic Social Teaching see J. Milburn Thompson, *Introducing Catholic Social Thought* (Maryknoll, NY: Orbis Books, 2010).

21 This association was popularized in William L. Shirer, *The Rise and Fall of the Third Reich: A History of Nazi Germany* (New York:

Touchstone, 1959). However, many scholars have criticized Shirer's link between Luther and the rise of Nazi power.

22 See, for examples, Wanda Deifelt, 'Advocacy, Political Participation, and Citizenship: Lutheran Contributions to Public Theology', *Dialog* 49 (2010): 108–14; and Uwe Siemon-Netto, 'Goodbye Utopia, Hello Luther! Half a millennium after the Protestant Reformation, American scholars seek advice from its leader', *The Atlantic Times* (December 2006).

23 See Michael Plekon, 'Eastern Orthodox Thought', in *The Blackwell Companion to Political Theology*; and Rowan Williams, ed., *Sergii Bulgakov: Towards a Russian Political Theology* (Edinburgh: T&T Clark, 1999).

24 See Daniel M. Bell, Jr., 'State and Civil Society', in *The Blackwell Companion to Political Theology*, 423–38; and Gaspar Martinez, *Confronting the Mystery of God: Political, Liberation and Public Theologies* (New York: Continuum, 2001).

25 Throughout this book, I refer to this specific movement as 'Political Theology' while referring to the field in general as 'political theology' to make this distinction clear.

26 For introductions to the political theologies of each of these authors, see the following: Richard Bauckham, *The Theology of Jürgen Moltmann* (London: T&T Clark, 1995); John K. Downey, ed., *Love's Strategy: The Political Theology of Johann Baptist Metz* (Harrisburg, PA: Trinity Press International, 1999); and Sarah H. Pinnock, ed., *The Theology of Dorothee Soelle* (Harrisburg, PA: Trinity Press International, 2003).

27 Bell, 'State and Civil Society', 429.

28 A distinction is often made between 'critical social theory' which has focused on sociological and political concerns and 'critical literary theory' which focused more on texts and hermeneutics. Today, critical theory is 'a corpus of changing and even conflicting ideas' which are joined to one another through their common 'continuing attention to specific social and textual practices and the anti-theory questions which enable critical theory both to proceed and glimpse its own provisional nature'. Graham Ward, *Theology and Contemporary Critical Theory*, 2nd edn (London: Macmillan Press Ltd., 2000), xviii.

29 See especially Johann Baptist Metz, *Faith in History and Society: Toward a Practical Fundamental Theology*, trans. J. Matthew Ashley (New York: Herder & Herder, 2007); *A Passion for God: The Mystical-Political Dimension of Christianity*, trans. J. Matthew Ashley (Mahwah, NJ: Paulist Press, 1998); and 'Political Theology',

in *Sacramentum Mundi: An Encyclopedia of Theology*, vol. V, ed. Karl Rahner (London: Burns & Oates, 1973).

30 See especially Jürgen Moltmann, *Religion, Revolution and the Future* (New York: Scribner, 1969); *On Human Dignity: Political Theology and Ethics* (Minneapolis: Augsburg Fortress Press, 1984); and his early theological trilogy, *Theology of Hope*, trans. J. Leitch (London: SCM, 1967); *The Crucified God*, trans. R. Wilson and J. Bowdon (London: SCM, 1974); and *The Church in the Power of the Spirit*, trans. M. Kohl (London: SCM, 1977).

31 See Dorothee Sölle, *Political Theology* (Philadelphia: Fortress Press, 1974) and *Against the Wind: Memoir of a Radical Christian* (Minneapolis: Augsburg Fortress, 1999).

32 Kirwan, 14.

33 Ibid., 138.

34 This was the stream of mid-twentieth century Catholic theology which called for movements both of *ressourcement*, or returning to the sources of scripture and the church fathers, as well as of *aggiornamento*, or openness to modernity and to dialogue between theology and the issues of contemporary life. This movement paved the way for and set the agenda for the issues discussed at the Second Vatican Council.

35 The 'theory of dependency' was developed as a denial of theories of modernization which interpreted countries and regions through a series of stages of development (thus 'developing' nations). This theory suggested that instead of being led through stages of development, these nations were actually trapped in relations of dependence upon wealthier nations. For a discussion of dependency theory in Liberation Theology and a bibliography on the topic, see Arthur F. McGovern, *Liberation Theology and Its Critics: Toward an Assessment* (Maryknoll, NY: Orbis Books, 1989).

36 Gustavo Gutiérrez, *A Theology of Liberation* (Maryknoll, NY: Orbis Books, 1973 and 1988).

37 For a recounting of the official responses and statements of the Roman Catholic Church to Liberation Theology, see Peter Hebblethwaite, 'Liberation Theology and the Roman Catholic Church', in *The Cambridge Companion to Liberation Theology* (Cambridge: Cambridge University Press, 2007): 209–28. These controversies were recently revisited by many when Cardinal Josef Ratzinger, who served as the Prefect for the Sacred Congregation for the Doctrine of the Faith during John Paul II's papacy, became Pope Benedict XVI.

38 We will consider some of the strengths and potential weaknesses of Liberation Theology through an introduction to the work of Marcella Althaus-Reid in Chapter 7.

39 James H. Cone, *Black Theology and Black Power* (Maryknoll, NY: Orbis Books, 1989), vii and 61. For his most recent work of Black Theology, see *The Cross and the Lynching Tree* (Maryknoll, NY: Orbis, 2011).

40 J. Deotis Roberts, *A Black Political Theology* (Louisville, KY: Westminster Press, 1974).

41 For examples of Feminist Theology from the global South see Chung Hyun Kyung, *Struggle to be the Sun Again: Introducing Asian Women's Theology* (Maryknoll, NY: Orbis, 1990); and Mercy Amba Oduyoye and Musimbi R. A. Kanyoro, eds, *The Will to Arise: Women, Tradition, and the Church in Africa* (Maryknoll, NY: Orbis Press, 1992).

42 See *Blessed Rage for Order: The New Pluralism in Theology* (New York: Seabury, 1975); and *The Analogical Imagination: Christian Theology and the Culture of Pluralism* (New York: Crossroad, 1981).

43 See Richard John Neuhaus, *The Naked Public Square: Religion and Democracy in America* (Grand Rapids: Eerdmans, 1984); and *The Catholic Moment: The Paradox of the Church in the Postmodern World* (New York: HarperCollins, 1990).

44 See John Courtney Murray, *Bridging the Sacred and the Secular: Selected Writings of John Courtney Murray*, ed. J. Leon Hooper (Washington, DC: Georgetown University Press, 1994); and Leon Hooper, *The Ethics of Discourse: The Social Ethics of John Courtney Murray* (Washington, DC: Georgetown University Press, 1986).

45 For a collection of essays on Public Theology which discusses the contributions of Stackhouse and gives a select bibliography of his works, see Deidre King Hainsworth and Scott R. Paeth, eds, *Public Theology for a Global Society: Essays in Honor of Max L. Stackhouse* (Grand Rapids: Eerdmans, 2010).

46 See Ronald F. Theimann, *Religion in Public Life: A Dilemma for Democracy* (Georgetown: Georgetown University Press/The Century Fund, 1996); and *Constructing a Public Theology: The Church in a Pluralistic Culture* (Louisville: Westminster-John Knox Press, 1991).

47 Max Stackhouse, 'Civil Religion, Political Theology and Public Theology: What's the Difference?' *Political Theology* 5.3 (2004): 288.

48 Ibid., 289.

49   Ibid., 291.

50   Martinez, 222.

51   Arne Rasmussen gives an in-depth comparison and contrast of the works of two specific first and second generation political theologians in *The Church as Polis: From Political Theology to Theological Politics as Exemplified by Jürgen Moltmann and Stanley Hauerwa*s (Notre Dame: University of Notre Dame Press, 1995).

52   Bell, 'State and Civil Society', 428–9.

53   Ibid., 433.

54   See for examples, William T. Cavanaugh, *Torture and Eucharist* (Oxford: Blackwell Publishing, 1998); and *Being Consumed: Economics and Christian Desire* (Grand Rapids: Eerdmans, 2008).

55   James K. A. Smith, *Introducing Radical Orthodoxy: Mapping a Post-secular Theology* (Grand Rapids: Baker Academic, 2004), 41–2.

56   The formative text which marked the beginning of the 'Yale School' was George A. Lindbeck, *The Nature of Doctrine: Religion and Theology in a Postliberal Age* (Louisville, KY: Westminster John Knox Press, 1984).

57   Especially Alasdair MacIntyre, *After Virtue* (Notre Dame: Notre Dame University Press, 1st edn, 1981 and 2nd edn, 1984); and *Whose Justice? Which Rationality?* (Notre Dame: Notre Dame University Press, 1988). Current philosophical interlocutors of Radical Orthodoxy include especially Giorgio Agamben and Slavoj Žižek.

58   See especially John Milbank, Catherine Pickstock and Graham Ward, eds, *Radical Orthodoxy* (London: Routledge, 1999); Creston Davis, John Milbank and Slavoj Žižek, eds, *Theology and the Political: The New Debate* (Durham, NC: Duke University Press, 2005); John Milbank, *The Future of Love: Essays in Political Theology* (Norwich: SCM Press, 2009); and Graham Ward, *Christ and Culture* (Oxford: Blackwell, 2005).

59   See for examples Naim Stifan Ateek, *Justice and Only Justice: A Palestinian Theology of Liberation* (Maryknoll, NY: Orbis, 1989); and Kim Yong Bock, ed., *Minjung Theology: People as the Subjects of History* (Singapore: Christian Conference of Asia, 1981).

60   See for examples Delores S. Williams, *Sisters in the Wilderness: The Challenge of Womanist God-Talk* (Maryknoll, NY: Orbis, 1993); and Emilie Townes, *Embracing the Spirit: Womanist Perspectives on Hope, Salvation and Transformation* (Maryknoll, NY: Orbis, 1997).

61   Gerard Loughlin, ed., *Queer Theology: Rethinking the Western Body* (Oxford: Blackwell, 2007).

62   Gerard Loughlin, 'Introduction', in *Queer Theology*, 7–8.

CHAPTER 3

1   I will chart this history in extreme brevity here. For a slightly more
    lengthy and in-depth introduction, see C. C. Pecknold, *Christianity
    and Politics: A Brief Guide to the History* (Eugene, OR: Cascade
    Books, 2010); for a significantly lengthier introduction see Michael
    Hoelzl and Graham Ward, eds, *Religion and Political Thought*
    (London: Continuum, 2006); and for a still more in-depth tracing of
    the history see Oliver O'Donovan and Joan Lockwood O'Donovan,
    eds, *From Irenaeus to Grotius: A Sourcebook in Christian Political
    Thought* (Grand Rapids: Eerdmans, 1999). Or for standard texts on
    specific historical periods, see Hugo Rahner, *Church and State in
    Early Christianity* (San Francisco: Ignatius Press, 1992); and John
    Neville Figgis, *Political Thought from Gerson to Grotius: 1414–1625*
    (New York: Harper, 1907).

2   We will see how and why this label has been challenged in Chapter 5.

3   Martin Luther, 'Address to the Christian Nobility of the German
    Nationality', in *Religion and Political Thought*, 70.

4   Ibid.

5   Ibid., 71.

6   Ibid.

7   All quotations below are from Martin Luther, 'On Secular Authority:
    How Far does the Obedience Owed to It Extend?' in Harro Höpfl,
    trans. and ed., *Luther and Calvin on Secular Authority* (Cambridge:
    Cambridge University Press, 1991), 3–43.

8   Ibid., 6.

9   Ibid., 12.

10 Ibid., 27.

11 For introductions to Bonhoeffer's life and thought, see John W. de
    Gruchy, ed., *The Cambridge Companion to Dietrich Bonhoeffer*
    (Cambridge: Cambridge University Press, 1999). For the authoritative
    biography, see Eberhard Bethge, *Dietrich Bonhoeffer: A Biography*
    (Minneapolis: Fortress, 2000). For a good place to begin reading his
    work, see Geffrey B. Kelly and F. Burton Nelson, eds, *A Testament to
    Freedom: The Essential Writings of Dietrich Bonhoeffer* (New York:
    HarperCollins, 1995).

12 For introductions to Barth's life and thought, see John Webster, ed.,
    The Cambridge Companion to Karl Barth (Cambridge: Cambridge
    University Press, 2000). For collections of his writings related to
    political theology see Clifford Green, ed., *Karl Barth: Theologian of*

Freedom (London: Collins Liturgical Publications, 1989); and David Haddorff, ed., *Community, State and Church: Three Essays by Karl Barth* (Eugene, OR: Wipf & Stock, 2004).

13 Karl Barth, *Theological Existence Today!: A Plea for Theological Freedom* (London: Hodder and Stoughton, 1933).

14 Bonhoeffer, Letter to Karl Barth (9 September 1933), in *No Rusty Swords: Letters, Lectures and Notes, 1928–1936, from the Collected Works of Dietrich Bonhoeffer,* vol. 1, ed. Edwin H. Robertson, trans. Edwin H. Robertson and John Bowden (London: Collins, 1965), 230.

15 Ibid.

16 Barth, Letter to Bonhoeffer (11 September 1933), in *No Rusty Swords*, 232.

17 Barth, Letter to Bonhoeffer (20 November 1933), in *No Rusty Swords*, 238–9.

18 Bonhoeffer, 'The Church and the Jewish Question', in *No Rusty Swords*, 222–4. It is more than a little ironic that Bonhoeffer opens this piece with two quotations from Luther's moments of irenic attitude towards Jews. Luther would also pen one of the most perniciously anti-Jewish documents of Christian history, *On the Jews and their Lies* (1543), in which he counselled such vicious treatment of Jews that the document was appealed to directly by Nazis.

19 Bonhoeffer, *No Rusty Swords*, 225.

20 Ibid.

21 Bonhoeffer, 'The Interpretation of the New Testament', in *No Rusty Swords*, 324.

22 Bonhoeffer, *Ethics*, ed. Eberhard Bethge (London: SCM Press, 1955), 303.

23 Ibid., 322.

24 Ibid., 323.

25 Ibid., 76–7.

26 The Barmen document is widely available online, and is also included in an extremely helpful collection for students of political theology: Andrew Bradstock and Christopher Rowland, eds, *Radical Christian Writings: A Reader* (Oxford: Blackwell, 2002), 201–3.

27 'The Barmen Declaration', in *Radical Christian Writings*, 202–3.

28 See Karl Barth, 'The Christian Community and the Civil Community', in Green, ed., *Karl Barth*, 265–96.

Chapter 4

1 While Yoder was a Mennonite throughout his life, Hauerwas has never been affiliated with an Anabaptist tradition ecclesially. He has been a Methodist most of his life and has more recently become Anglican.

2 See especially Albert Schweitzer, *The Quest of the Historical Jesus*, first published in 1906, translated into English in 1910 by W. Montgomery.

3 The characteristic texts of this phase of the quest include John Dominic Crossan, *The Historical Jesus: The Life of a Mediterranean Jewish Peasant* (San Francisco: HarperCollins, 1991); and John P. Meier, *A Marginal Jew: Rethinking the Historical Jesus* (Garden City, NY: Doubleday, 1992).

4 See Ernst Bammel and C. F. D. Moule, eds, *Jesus and the Politics of His Day* (Cambridge: Cambridge University Press, 1984).

5 See for examples, Ched Myers, *Binding the Strongman: A Political Reading of Mark's Story of Jesus* (Maryknoll, NY: Orbis, 1988 and 2008); and Richard A. Horsley, *Jesus and Empire: The Kingdom of God and the New World Disorder* (Minneapolis: Augsburg Fortress, 2003).

6 For a very accessible though notably pro-Anabaptist historical introduction see William R. Estep, *The Anabaptist Story: An Introduction to Sixteenth-Century Anabaptism*, 3rd edn (Grand Rapids: William B. Eerdmans, 1996). For an introduction which is less sympathetic but not hostile, and slightly more dense see Hans-Jürgen Goertz, *The Anabaptists*, trans. Trevor Johnson (London: Routledge, 1996).

7 'The Schleitheim Brotherly Union', in John Howard Yoder, trans. and ed., *The Legacy of Michael Sattler* (Scottdale, PA: Herald Press, 1973), 39–40.

8 Ibid., 40.

9 Ibid.

10 Ibid.

11 Ibid., 39.

12 Yoder, *The Politics of Jesus*, 11.

13 Ibid., 10.

14 Ibid., 36.

15 Ibid., 51.

16 This argument is made in separate places throughout *The Politics of Jesus*, and is made more succinctly in 'The Original Revolution',

which was published in *The Original Revolution* as well as *For the Nations.*

17 See Yoder, *The Politics of Jesus*, chapter 6.

18 Ibid., 105.

19 Ibid., 107.

20 Ibid., 106.

21 Ibid., 107.

22 Ibid., 236–7.

23 Ibid., 235–6.

24 Ibid., 234.

25 Ibid., 237.

26 Ibid., 246.

27 For a biography, see Richard Wightman Fox, *Reinhold Niebuhr: A Biography* (Ithaca, NY: Cornell University Press, 1986); for a good place to begin reading his work, see Robert McAfee Brown, ed., *The Essential Reinhold Niebuhr: Selected Essays and Addresses* (New Haven, CT: Yale University Press, 1986); and for a recent collection of contemporary political theologians reflecting on his legacy, see Richard Harries and Stephen Platten, eds, *Reinhold Niebuhr and Contemporary Politics: God and Power* (Oxford: Oxford University Press, 2010).

28 A must-read for students of political theology is H. Richard Niebuhr's classic work, *Christ and Culture* (New York: Harper, 1951). While Reinhold has been influential for Public Theology, H. Richard has been more influential for Postliberalism. For one of the most discussed examples of their differences and interaction, see their debate about US non-involvement in world war in the articles H. Richard Niebuhr, 'The Grace of Doing Nothing', and 'The Only Way into the Kingdom of God', and Reinhold Niebuhr, 'Must We Do Nothing?'. These were printed in the March and April 1932 issues of *Christian Century*, and are now more readily available in Wayne G. Boulton, Thomas D. Kennedy and Allen Verhey, eds, *From Christ to the World: Introductory Readings in Christian Ethics* (Grand Rapids: Eerdmans, 1994), 419–27.

29 In this portion of his theory, the influence of Søren Kierkegaard is clear.

30 See especially Reinhold Niebuhr, *Moral Man and Immoral Society: A Study of Ethics and Politics* (Louisville, KY: Westminster John Knox Press, 2001).

31 Reinhold Niebuhr, *Love and Justice: Selections from the Shorter Writings of Reinhold Niebuhr*, ed. D. B. Robertson (Louisville, KY: Westminster/John Knox Press, 1957).

32 Niebuhr, 'Justice and Love', in *Love and Justice*, 28.

33 Niebuhr, 'The Ethic of Jesus and the Social Problem', in *Love and Justice*, 30.

34 Ibid., 30.

35 Ibid., 33.

36 Ibid., 30.

37 Ibid.

38 Ibid., 33.

39 Ibid., 32.

40 Niebuhr, 'Justice and Love', 29.

41 Niebuhr, 'The Ethic of Jesus and the Social Problem', 38.

42 Part IV: 'Love and Justice and the Pacifist Issue', 241–302.

43 Originally published in the United Kingdom as a pamphlet from SCM Press (1940). Now easily accessible online and in *The Essential Reinhold Niebuhr*, 102–19.

44 Reinhold Niebuhr, 'Why the Christian Church Is Not Pacifist', in *The Essential Reinhold Niebuhr,* 106.

45 Ibid., 113.

46 Ibid.

47 Ibid., 103.

48 Ibid., 115.

49 Ibid., 107.

50 Ibid., 105.

51 Ibid., 119.

52 Ibid., 104.

53 Ibid.

54 Ibid., 107.

CHAPTER 5

1 For an extremely accessible introduction to war and peace in the Christian tradition, see the provocatively titled: Mark J. Allman, *Who Would Jesus Kill? War, Peace and the Christian Tradition* (Winona, MN: St Mary's Press, 2008).

2 Justin Martyr, *Dialogue with Trypho*, trans. Thomas B. Falls (Washington, DC: The Catholic University of America Press, 2003), chapter 110, Section 3.

3 See Clement of Alexandria, *Protrepticus*.

4 Tertullian, *On the Crown*, 11.1-7. See Louis J. Swift, *The Early Fathers on War and Military Service* (Wilmington, DE: Michael Glazier, Inc., 1983), 43–4.

5 The Catholic Worker Movement and Dorothy Day deserve their own section and are one of the most lamentable exclusions from this book due to limitations of length and scope. On Dorothy Day see Jim Forest, *Love is the Measure: A Biography of Dorothy Day* (Maryknoll, NY: Orbis, 1994); and Robert Ellsberg, ed., *Dorothy Day: Selected Writings* (Maryknoll, NY: Orbis, 1983). On the Catholic Worker Movement see Mark Zwick and Louise Zwick, *The Catholic Worker Movement: Intellectual and Spiritual Origins* (Mahwah, NJ: Paulist Press, 2005).

6 For two brief pieces which serve to introduce pacifism in Yoder and Hauerwas see Yoder, 'Peace without Eschatology?', and Hauerwas, 'Peacemaking: The Virtue of the Church (1985)' in *The Hauerwas Reader*, ed. John Berkman and Michael Cartwright (Durham, NC: Duke University Press, 2001), 318–26.

7 Augustine, *Reply to Faustus the Manichaean*, in *The Nicene and Post-Nicene Fathers*, vol. IV, trans. Richard Stothert (Peabody, MA: Hendrickson, 1994), Book XXII, chapter 74.

8 Aquinas, *Summa Theologiae*, IaIIae. 40. 1. *responsio*.

9 See Daniel M. Bell, Jr., *Just War as Christian Discipleship: Recentering the Tradition in the Church rather than the State* (Grand Rapids: Brazos Press, 2009), 15–16.

10 Jean Bethke Elshtain, 'Augustine', in *The Blackwell Companion to Political Theology*, 44.

11 See pages 27–8 above.

12 See note 62, page 162 above.

13 Augustine, *Letter 93*, in *The Nicene and Post-Nicene Fathers*, vol. I, trans. J. G. Cunningham (Peabody, MA: Hendrickson, 1994), chapter 3.9.

14 Ibid., chapter 5.16.

15 See pages 37–8 above.

16 See John Milbank, *Theology and Social Theory*, especially chapters 10 and 12.

17 Ibid., 393.

18 Ibid., 393–4. He quotes Augustine, *City of God*, Book IV, chapter 15.

19 Milbank, *Theology and Social Theory*, 394. He refers especially to Book XIV, chapter 17; and Book XIX, chapters 10, 13 and 27.

20 See ibid., 438–40.

21 Smith, *Introducing Radical Orthodoxy*, 196–7.

22 Cavanaugh, *Torture and Eucharist*.

23 Cavanaugh, *The Myth of Religious Violence* (Oxford: Oxford University Press, 2009).

24 Cavanaugh, *Theopolitical Imagination* (Edinburgh: T&T Clark, 2002).

25 Cavanaugh, *The Myth of Religious Violence*, 3.

26 Ibid., 121.

27 Ibid., 55.

28 Ibid., 56.

29 Liberalism and the liberal state will be discussed in Chapter 6.

30 Ibid., 4.

31 Her books include *Augustine and the Limits of Politics* (Notre Dame: University of Notre Dame Press, 1996); and *Public Man, Private Woman: Women in Social and Political Thought* (Princeton: Princeton University Press, 1981).

32 Jean Bethke Elshtain, *Just War against Terror: The Burden of American Power in a Violent World* (New York: Basic Books, 2003).

33 Ibid., 46.

34 Ibid., 48.

35 Ibid., 49.

36 She says of Hobbes and the 'war of all against all' that 'Hobbes overstated his case. But there is a powerful element of truth in his depiction of the state of nature.' Ibid., 48.

37 For Elshtain on Niebuhr see especially pages 106–11.

38 Ibid., 3 and 5.

39 Ibid., 159.

40 Ibid., 57.

41 Ibid., 58.

42 Ibid., 59.

43 Ibid., 61.

44 Ibid., 58.

45 Ibid., 61.

46 Ibid., 58.

47 Ibid., 61.

48 Ibid.

49 Ibid., 58.

50 Ibid., 62.

51 Ibid., 65.

52 Ibid.

53 Elshtain, 'Stay in Afghanistan? There's No Other Choice', *Christianity Today* 54:9 (September 2010): 72–3.

54 Elshtain, *Just War against Terror*, 2004 edition, 182–92.

55 Ibid., 189.

56 Ibid., 192.

57 Ibid., 167.

58 Ibid., 168.

59 Ibid., 173.

60 Milbank describes his agreement and disagreement with Yoder and Hauerwas on pacifism in 'Power is Necessary for Peace: In Defence of Constantine', ABC Religion and Ethics (29 October 2010, updated 1 November 2010), http://www.abc.net.au/religion/articles/2010/10/29/3051980.htm, accessed 20 September 2011.

Chapter 6

1 The following is based on a lengthier introduction to types and characteristics of liberalism in Robert Song, *Christianity and Liberal Society* (Oxford: Oxford University Press, 1997), especially pages 37–48. Song's book is a helpful introduction to liberalism and various theological employments of liberalism.

2 Important exceptions include Robert Song (see note 1, above); Christopher Insole, *The Politics of Human Frailty: A Theological Defence of Liberalism* (London: SCM Press, 2004); and Eric Gregory, discussed below.

3   Smith, *Introducing Radical Orthodoxy*, 71.

4   Milbank, 'The Programme of Radical Orthodoxy', in *Radical Orthodoxy? A Catholic Enquiry*, ed. Laurance Paul Hemming (Burlington, VA: Ashgate, 2000), 45.

5   For introductions to Hauerwas's life and work see Stanley Hauerwas, *Hannah's Child: A Theologian's Memoir* (Grand Rapids: Eerdmans, 2010); and *The Hauerwas Reader*.

6   Stanley Hauerwas, 'A Christian Critique of Christian America', in *The Hauerwas Reader*, 459–80.

7   Stanley Hauerwas, 'The Church and Liberal Democracy: The Moral Limits of a Secular Polity', in *A Community of Character: Toward a Constructive Christian Social Ethic* (Notre Dame: Notre Dame University Press, 1981).

8   John Berkman, 'Introduction to the Hauerwas Reader', in *The Hauerwas Reader*, 8.

9   Hauerwas, 'The Church and Liberal Democracy', 78.

10 Ibid.

11 For a series of essays on the history and legacy of the Social Gospel Movement, see Christopher H. Evans, ed., *The Social Gospel Today* (Louisville, KY: Westminster John Knox Press, 2001).

12 See pages 84–8 above.

13 Hauerwas, 'The Church and Liberal Democracy', 73.

14 Hauerwas, 'A Christian Critique of Christian America', 467.

15 John Rawls, *A Theory of Justice* (Cambridge, MA: Harvard University Press, 1971).

16 Hauerwas, 'A Christian Critique of Christian America', 470.

17 Ibid., 471.

18 Hauerwas, 'The Church and Liberal Democracy', 78.

19 Ibid.

20 Ibid., 80.

21 Ibid., 82.

22 Ibid.

23 Hauerwas, 'A Christian Critique of Christian America', 477.

24 Hauerwas, 'The Church and Liberal Democracy', 83.

25 Ibid., 84.

26 See pages 16–17 above.

27 Hauerwas, 'A Christian Critique of Christian America', 476.

28 Hauerwas, 'The Church and Liberal Democracy', 84.

29 Ibid., 84–5.

30 Ibid., 86.

31 Hauerwas, 'A Christian Critique of Christian America', 477.

32 Hauerwas, 'The Church and Liberal Democracy', 85.

33 John Milbank, 'Liberality versus Liberalism', in *The Future of Love: Essays in Political Theology* (London: SCM Press, 2009), 242–63.

34 Ibid., 243.

35 Ibid., 246.

36 Ibid., 244.

37 Ibid., 252–3.

38 Milbank, *Theology and Social Theory*, 403.

39 Ibid., 410.

40 Ibid., 407.

41 Milbank, 'Liberality versus Liberalism', 245.

42 Milbank, *Theology and Social Theory*, 413.

43 Milbank, 'Liberality versus Liberalism', 249–50. The '(*sic*)' was inserted by Milbank.

44 Ibid., 245.

45 Ibid., 242.

46 Ibid., 246.

47 Eric Gregory, *Politics and the Order of Love: An Ethic of Democratic Citizenship* (Chicago: University of Chicago Press, 2008), 370.

48 Ibid., 1.

49 Ibid., 23.

50 Ibid., 12.

51 Ibid., 19.

52 Ibid., 8.

53 Ibid., 8 and 9.

54 His feminist interlocutors include Carol Gilligan, Joan C. Tronto, Eve Fedder Kittay and Martha Nussbaum.

55 Gregory, 379.

56 Ibid.

57 Ibid., 17.

58 Ibid., 9.

59 Ibid., 369.

60 Ibid., 4.

61 Ibid., 9.

62 Ibid., 18.

63 Ibid., 28.

64 Ibid., 9

65 Ibid.

66 Ibid., 19.

67 Another important aspect is his argument concerning what is meant by and should be made of Augustine's references to 'using the world' and 'enjoying God'. This enters into a debate too technical to treat adequately here, but those wanting to understand Gregory, and especially to compare and contrast his Augustinianism with that of Milbank, will need to read further here. The debate began with Anders Nygren, *Agape and Eros* (Philadelphia: Westminster, 1953). For an introduction to Nygren and the reception of his work, see William Werpehowski, 'Anders Nygren's *Agape and Eros*', in *The Oxford Handbook of Theological Ethics*, ed. Gilbert Mileander and William Werpehowski (Oxford: Oxford University Press), 433–48.

68 Gregory, 15.

69 Ibid., 125. Interestingly, after noting the alignment of Yoder, Hauerwas and Milbank on this point, Gregory then dismisses Yoder and Hauerwas from the conversation because their rejection of liberalism is 'governed by a pacifist stance against the coercive use of force in political life', as if it is thereby obvious why their work need not detain him further. This is a familiar trope in non-pacifist political theology, where authors often feel at liberty to assume the irrelevance of pacifism to politics. For an interesting instance, see the conversation between Hauerwas and the editors of *First Things* when Hauerwas resigned from the editorial board after they published their conviction that pacifists could have no voice in the discussion of the use of military force in response to the attacks of September 11, 2001. Stanley Hauerwas and The Editors, 'In a Time of War: An Exchange', *First Things* 120 (February 2002): 11–15.

70 Gregory, 24.

71 Ibid., 78.

72 Ibid., 140–1.

73 Ibid., 364.

CHAPTER 7

1   Martin Luther King, Jr, 'Letter from a Birmingham Jail', in *A Testament of Hope: The Essential Writings of Martin Luther King, Jr.*, ed. James Melvin Washington (San Francisco: Harper & Row, 1986), 289–302.

2   King, *Where Do We Go From Here: Chaos or Community?* in *A Testament of Hope*, 555–633.

3   King, 'A Time to Break Silence', in *A Testament of Hope*, 234.

4   Ibid.

5   Ibid., 233.

6   Ibid., 238.

7   Ibid., 240.

8   Ibid., 241.

9   See Rosemary Radford Ruether, *Faith and Fratricide: The Theological Roots of Anti-Semitism* (New York: Seabury Press, 1974); and Rosemary Radford Ruether and Herman J. Ruether, *The Wrath of Jonah: The Crisis of Religious Nationalism in the Israeli-Palestinian Conflict* (Minneapolis: Augsburg Fortress, 2002).

10 Rosemary Radford Ruether, *Sexism and God-Talk: Toward a Feminist Theology* (Boston, MA: Beacon Press, 1993), 214. For her most recent work on political theology, see *Christianity and Social Systems: Historical Constructions and Ethical Challenges* (Lanham, MD: Rowman & Littlefield, 2009).

11 Ruether, *Sexism and God-Talk*, 221.

12 Ibid.

13 Ibid., 224.

14 Ibid., 226.

15 Ibid., 228.

16 Ibid., 231.

17 Ibid., 232–33.

18 Ibid., 233.

19 Ibid., xv.

20 Ruether, *Gaia and God: An Ecofeminist Theology of Earth Healing* (London: SCM Press, 1992), 2.

21 Ibid.

22 Ibid., 3.

23 Ibid., 4.

24 Ibid., 255.

25 Ibid., chapter ten, 'Creating a Healed World', 254–74.

26 See Marcella Althaus-Reid, *Indecent Theology: Theological Perversions in Sex, Gender and Politics* (Abingdon: Routledge, 2000).

27 Marcella Althaus-Reid, 'What is Indecent Theology? Why *Indecent?*' on http://www.althaus-reid.com/IT.html, accessed 30 August 2011.

28 Marcella Althaus-Reid, 'Graffiti on the Walls of the Cathedral of Buenos Aires: Doing Theology, Love and Politics at the Margins', in *Religion and Political Thought*, 243.

29 Ibid., 244.

30 Ibid., 247.

31 Ibid., 251.

32 Ibid., 252.

33 Ibid., 257.

34 Ibid., 256.

CHAPTER 8

1 Jürgen Moltmann, *The Spirit of Life: A Universal Affirmation*, trans. M. Kohl (London: SCM, 1992).

2 Mark Lewis Taylor, 'Spirit', in *The Blackwell Companion to Political Theology,* 377–92.

3 Robert Beckford, *Dread and Pentecostal: A Political Theology for the Black Church in Britain* (London: SPCK, 2000).

4 For histories of such movements, see Stephen Hunt, ed., *Christian Millenarianism: From the Early Church to Waco* (Bloomington, IN: Indiana University Press, 2001); and Norman Cohn, *The Pursuit of the Millennium: Revolutionary Millenarians and Mystical Anarchists of the Middle Ages* (Oxford: Oxford University Press, 1970).

5 Nathan R. Kerr, *Christ, History and Apocalyptic: The Politics of Christian Mission* (Eugene, OR: Cascade Books, 2009), 2.

6 Ibid., 168.

7 Charles Mathewes, *A Theology of Public Life* (Cambridge: Cambridge University Press, 2007), 2.

8 Kerr, 2.

9 Ibid., 161–2.

10 Ibid., 191.

11 Mathewes, 39.

12 Ibid., 15.

13 Ibid., 17.

14 Ibid., 26.

15 Ibid., 146.

16 Ibid., 26.

17 I have written on this piece elsewhere in relation to the apocalypticism of American Christian Zionism. See Elizabeth Phillips, '"We've Read the End of the Book": An Engagement with Contemporary Christian Zionism through the Eschatology of John Howard Yoder', *Studies in Christian Ethics* 21.3 (2008): 342–61.

18 Yoder, 'Armaments and Eschatology', *Studies in Christian Ethics* 1:1 (1988): 53.

19 Ibid.

20 Ibid. In one place Yoder structures an entire presentation/essay around this theme. 'To Serve Our God and to Rule the World' describes nine implications of seeing history doxologically.

21 Rowan Williams, 'Ascension Day', in *Open to Judgement* (London: Darton, Longman & Todd, 1994), 84.

22 Ibid., 85.

23 For an excellent collection of essays which further explore many of these aspects of Thomas – though one which is not for beginning theologians – see Rik Van Nieuwenhove and Joseph Wawryow, eds, *The Theology of Thomas Aquinas* (Notre Dame: University of Notre Dame Press, 2005).

24 Michael Hoelzl and Graham Ward, 'Thomas Aquinas', in *Religion and Political Thought*, 40.

25 See for example Susanne M. DeCrane, *Aquinas, Feminism and the Common Good* (Washington, DC: Georgetown University Press, 2004).

26 Mark Jordan, *Rewritten Theology: Aquinas after His Readers* (Oxford: Blackwell, 2006), 17.

BIBLIOGRAPHY

Allman, Mark J. *Who Would Jesus Kill? War, Peace and the Christian Tradition* (Winona, MN: St Mary's Press, 2008).

Althaus-Reid, Marcella. 'Graffiti on the Walls of the Cathedral of Buenos Aires: Doing Theology, Love and Politics at the Margins', in *Religion and Political Thought*, ed. Michael Hoelzl and Graham Ward (London: Continuum, 2006), 243–58.

—. *Indecent Theology: Theological Perversions in Sex, Gender and Politics* (London: Routledge, 2000).

—. 'What is Indecent Theology? Why Indecent?', http://www.althaus-reid.com/IT.html, accessed 30 August 2011.

Aquinas. *Political Writings*, trans. and ed. R. W. Dyson (Cambridge: Cambridge University Press, 2002).

Aristotle. *The Politics*, trans. Ernest Barker (Oxford: Oxford University Press, 1995).

Ateek, Naim Stifan. *Justice and Only Justice: A Palestinian Theology of Liberation* (Maryknoll, NY: Orbis, 1989).

Augustine. *City of God*, trans. Henry Bettenson (London: Penguin Books, 1972).

—. Letter 93, in *The Nicene and Post-Nicene Fathers*, vol. I, trans. J. G. Cunningham (Peabody, MA: Hendrickson, 1994).

—. 'Reply to Faustus the Manichaean', in *The Nicene and Post-Nicene Fathers*, vol. IV, trans. Richard Stothert (Peabody, MA: Hendrickson, 1994).

Bammel, Ernst and C. F. D. Moule, eds. *Jesus and the Politics of His Day* (Cambridge: Cambridge University Press, 1984).

Barth, Karl. *Theological Existence Today!: A Plea for Theological Freedom* (London: Hodder and Stoughton, 1933).

Barth, Karl. *Community, State and Church: Three Essays by Karl Barth*, ed. David Haddorff (Eugene, OR: Wipf & Stock, 2004).

Bauckham, Richard. *The Theology of Jürgen Moltmann* (London: T&T Clark, 1995).

Bauerschmidt, Frederick Christian. 'Aquinas', in *The Blackwell Companion to Political Theology* (Oxford: Blackwell, 2004), 48–61.

Beckford, Robert. *Dread and Pentecostal: A Political Theology for the Black Church in Britain* (London: SPCK, 2000).

Bell, Daniel M. *Just War as Christian Discipleship: Recentering the Tradition in the Church rather than the State* (Grand Rapids: Brazos Press, 2009).

—. 'State and Civil Society', in *The Blackwell Companion to Political Theology* (Oxford: Blackwell, 2004), 423–38.

Bellah, Robert N. and Steven M. Tipton, eds. *The Robert Bellah Reader* (Durham, NC: Duke University Press, 2006).

Berger, Peter, Grace Davie and Effie Fokas. *Religious America, Secular Europe? A Theme and Variation* (Aldershot: Ashgate, 2008).

Berkman, John. 'Introduction to the Hauerwas Reader', in *The Hauerwas Reader* (Durham, NC: Duke University Press, 2001), 3–16.

Bethge, Eberhard. *Dietrich Bonhoeffer: A Biography* (Minneapolis: Fortress, 2000).

Black, Antony. *The History of Islamic Political Thought* (Edinburgh: Edinburgh University Press, 2001).

Bock, Kim Yong, ed. *Minjung Theology: People as the Subjects of History* (Singapore: Christian Conference of Asia, 1981).

Bonhoeffer, Dietrich. *Ethics*, ed. Eberhard Bethge (London: SCM Press, 1955).

—. *No Rusty Swords: Letters, Lectures and Notes, 1928–1936, from the Collected Works of Dietrich Bonhoeffer*, vol. 1, ed. Edwin H. Robertson, trans. Edwin H. Robertson and John Bowden (London: Collins, 1965).

Boulton, Wayne G., Thomas D. Kennedy and Allen Verhey, eds. *From Christ to the World: Introductory Readings in Christian Ethics* (Grand Rapids: Eerdmans, 1994).

Bradstock, Andrew and Christopher Rowland, eds. *Radical Christian Writings: A Reader* (Oxford: Blackwell, 2002).

Bretherton, Luke. 'Introduction: Oliver O'Donovan's Political Theology and the Liberal Imperative', *Political Theology* 9.3 (2008): 265–71.

Brueggemann, Walter. 'Scripture: Old Testament', in *The Blackwell Companion to Political Theology* (Oxford: Blackwell, 2004), 7–20.

Cavanaugh, William T. *Being Consumed: Economics and Christian Desire* (Grand Rapids: Eerdmans, 2008).

—. *Migrations of the Holy: God, State, and the Political Meaning of the Church* (Grand Rapids: Eerdmans, 2011).

—. *The Myth of Religious Violence* (Oxford: Oxford University Press, 2009).

—. *Theopolitical Imagination* (Edinburgh: T&T Clark, 2002).

—. *Torture and Eucharist* (Oxford: Blackwell Publishing, 1998).

Cohn, Norman. *The Pursuit of the Millennium: Revolutionary Millenarians and Mystical Anarchists of the Middle Ages* (Oxford: Oxford University Press, 1970).

Cone, James H. *Black Theology and Black Power* (Maryknoll, NY: Orbis, 1989).

—. *The Cross and the Lynching Tree* (Maryknoll, NY: Orbis, 2011).

Crossan, John Dominic. *The Historical Jesus: The Life of a Mediterranean Jewish Peasant* (San Francisco: Harper/Collins, 1991).

Davis, Creston. 'Political Theology – The Continental Shift', *Political Theology* 11.1 (2010): 5–14.

Davis, Creston, John Milbank and Slavoj Žižek, eds. *Theology and the Political: The New Debate* (Durham, NC: Duke University Press, 2005).

Dawkins, Richard. *A Devil's Chaplain: Reflections on Hope, Lies, Science, and Love* (London: Weidenfeld and Nicolson, 2003).

Day, Dorothy. *Dorothy Day: Selected Writings*, ed. Robert Ellsberg (Maryknoll, NY: Orbis, 1983).

DeCrane, Susanne M. *Aquinas, Feminism and the Common Good* (Washington, DC: Georgetown University Press, 2004).

Deifelt, Wanda. 'Advocacy, Political Participation, and Citizenship: Lutheran Contributions to Public Theology', *Dialog* 49 (2010): 108–14.

Downey, John K., ed. *Love's Strategy: The Political Theology of Johann Baptist Metz* (Harrisburg, PA: Trinity Press International, 1999).

Dyson, R. W. 'Introduction', in *St Thomas Aquinas: Political Writings* (Cambridge: Cambridge University Press, 2002), xvii–xxxvi.

Elshtain, Jean Bethke. 'Augustine', in *The Blackwell Companion to Political Theology* (Oxford: Blackwell, 2004), 35–47.

—. *Augustine and the Limits of Politics* (Notre Dame: University of Notre Dame Press, 1996).

—. *Just War against Terror: The Burden of American Power in a Violent World* (New York: Basic Books, 2004 [2003]).

—. *Public Man, Private Woman: Women in Social and Political Thought* (Princeton: Princeton University Press, 1981).

—. 'Stay in Afghanistan? There's No Other Choice', *Christianity Today* 54:9 (September 2010): 72–3.

Estep, William R. *The Anabaptist Story: An Introduction to Sixteenth-Century Anabaptism*, 3rd edn (Grand Rapids: William B. Eerdmans, 1996).

Evans, Christopher H., ed. *The Social Gospel Today* (Louisville, KY: Westminster John Knox Press, 2001).

Figgis, John Neville. *Political Thought from Gerson to Grotius: 1414–1625* (New York: Harper, 1907).

Finnis, John. *Natural Law and Natural Rights*, 2nd edn (New York: Oxford University Press, 2011).

Forest, Jim. *Love is the Measure: A Biography of Dorothy Day* (Maryknoll, NY: Orbis, 1994).

Fox, Richard Wightman. *Reinhold Niebuhr: A Biography* (Ithaca, NY: Cornell University Press, 1986).

Goertz, Hans-Jürgen. *The Anabaptists*, trans. Trevor Johnson (London: Routledge, 1996).

Green, Clifford, ed. *Karl Barth: Theologian of Freedom* (London: Collins Liturgical Publications, 1989).

Gregory, Eric. *Politics and the Order of Love: An Ethic of Democratic Citizenship* (Chicago: University of Chicago Press, 2008).

de Gruchy, John W., ed. *The Cambridge Companion to Dietrich Bonhoeffer* (Cambridge: Cambridge University Press, 1999).

Gutiérrez, Gustavo. *A Theology of Liberation* (Maryknoll: Orbis Books, 1988 [1973]).

Hainsworth, Deidre King and Scott R. Paeth, eds. *Public Theology for a Global Society: Essays in Honor of Max L. Stackhouse* (Grand Rapids: Eerdmans, 2010).

Harries, Richard and Stephen Platten, eds. *Reinhold Niebuhr and Contemporary Politics: God and Power* (Oxford: Oxford University Press, 2010).

Hauerwas, Stanley. *A Community of Character: Toward a Constructive Christian Social Ethic* (Notre Dame: Notre Dame University Press, 1981).

—. *Hannah's Child: A Theologian's Memoir* (Grand Rapids: Eerdmans, 2010).

—. *The Hauerwas Reader*, ed. John Berkman and Michael Cartwright (Durham, NC: Duke University Press, 2001).

Hauerwas, Stanley and The Editors. 'In a Time of War: An Exchange', *First Things* 120 (February 2002): 11–15.

Hebblethwaite, Peter. 'Liberation Theology and the Roman Catholic Church', in *The Cambridge Companion to Liberation Theology* (Cambridge: Cambridge University Press, 2007): 209–28.

Hobbes, Thomas. *Leviathan: Revised Student Edition*, ed. Richard Tuck (Cambridge: Cambridge University Press, 1996).

Hoelzl, Michael and Graham Ward, eds. *Religion and Political Thought* (London: Continuum, 2006).

Hollerich, Michael. 'Carl Schmitt', in *The Blackwell Companion to Political Theology* (Oxford: Blackwell, 2004), 107–22.

Hooper, Leon. *The Ethics of Discourse: The Social Ethics of John Courtney Murray* (Washington, DC: Georgetown University Press, 1986).

Horsley, Richard A. *Jesus and Empire: The Kingdom of God and the New World Disorder* (Minneapolis: Augsburg Fortress, 2003).

Hunt, Stephen, ed. *Christian Millenarianism: From the Early Church to Waco* (Bloomington, IN: Indiana University Press, 2001).

Insole, Christopher. *The Politics of Human Frailty: A Theological Defence of Liberalism* (London: SCM Press, 2004).

Jordan, Mark. *Rewritten Theology: Aquinas after His Readers* (Oxford: Blackwell, 2006).

Juergensmeyer, Mark. *Terror in the Mind of God: The Global Rise of Religious Violence* (Berkeley: University of California Press, 2003).

Kelly, Geffrey B. and F. Burton Nelson, eds. *A Testament to Freedom: The Essential Writings of Dietrich Bonhoeffer* (New York: HarperCollins, 1995).

Kerr, Nathan R. *Christ, History and Apocalyptic: The Politics of Christian Mission* (Eugene, OR: Cascade Books, 2009).

Khir, Bustami Mohamed. 'The Islamic Quest for Sociopolitical Justice', in *The Blackwell Companion to Political Theology* (Oxford: Blackwell, 2004), 503–18.

King, Martin Luther, Jr. *A Testament of Hope: The Essential Writings of Martin Luther King, Jr.*, ed. James Melvin Washington (San Francisco: Harper & Row, 1986).

Kirwan, Michael. *Political Theology: A New Introduction* (London: Darton, Longman & Todd, 2008).

Kyung, Chung Hyun. *Struggle to be the Sun Again: Introducing Asian Women's Theology* (Maryknoll, NY: Orbis, 1990).

Lindbeck, George A. *The Nature of Doctrine: Religion and Theology in a Postliberal Age* (Louisville, KY: Westminster John Knox Press, 1984).

Long, D. Stephen. 'What Makes Theology "Political"? "Come Let us Reason Together"', *Political Theology* 5:4 (2004): 393–409.

Loughlin, Gerard, ed. *Queer Theology: Rethinking the Western Body* (Oxford: Blackwell, 2007).

Luther, Martin. 'Address to the Christian Nobility of the German Nationality', in *Religion and Political Thought*, ed. Michael Hoelzl and Graham Ward (London: Continuum, 2006), 68–73.

—. 'On Secular Authority: How Far does the Obedience Owed to it Extend?', in *Luther and Calvin on Secular Authority*, trans. and ed. Harro Höpfl (Cambridge: Cambridge University Press, 1991): 3–43.

MacIntyre, Alasdair. *After Virtue* (Notre Dame: Notre Dame University Press, 1984 [1981]).

—. *Whose Justice? Which Rationality?* (Notre Dame: Notre Dame University Press, 1988).

Markus, R. A. *Saeculum: History and Society in the Theology of St Augustine* (Cambridge: Cambridge University Press, 1970).

Martinez, Gaspar. *Confronting the Mystery of God: Political, Liberation and Public Theologies* (New York: Continuum, 2001).

Mathewes, Charles. *A Theology of Public Life* (Cambridge: Cambridge University Press, 2007).

McGovern, Arthur F. *Liberation Theology and Its Critics: Toward an Assessment* (Maryknoll, NY: Orbis Books, 1989).

Meier, John P. *A Marginal Jew: Rethinking the Historical Jesus* (Garden City, NY: Doubleday, 1992).

Metz, Johann Baptist. *Faith in History and Society: Toward a Practical Fundamental Theology*, trans. J. Matthew Ashley (New York: Herder & Herder, 2007).

—. *A Passion for God: The Mystical-Political Dimension of Christianity*, trans. J. Matthew Ashley (Mahwah, NJ: Paulist Press, 1998).

—. 'Political Theology', in *Sacramentum Mundi: An Encyclopedia of Theology*, vol. V, ed. Karl Rahner (London: Burns & Oates, 1973).

Milbank, John. *The Future of Love: Essays in Political Theology* (Norwich: SCM Press, 2009).

—. 'Power is Necessary for Peace: In Defence of Constantine', *ABC Religion and Ethics* (29 October 2010, updated 1 November 2010), http://www.abc.net.au/religion/articles/2010/10/29/3051980.htm, accessed 20 September 2011.

—. 'The Programme of Radical Orthodoxy', in *Radical Orthodoxy? A Catholic Enquiry*, ed. Laurence Paul Hemming (Burlington, VA: Ashgate, 2000), 33–45.

—. *Theology and Social Theory: Beyond Secular Reason* (Oxford: Blackwell Publishing, 1990).

Milbank, John, Catherine Pickstock and Graham Ward, eds. *Radical Orthodoxy* (London: Routledge, 1999).

Milbank, John, Slavoj Žižek and Creston Davis. *Paul's New Moment: Continental Philosophy and the Future of Christian Theology* (Grand Rapids: Brazos Press, 2010).

Moltmann, Jürgen. *The Church in the Power of the Spirit*, trans. M. Kohl (London: SCM, 1977).

—. 'Covenant or Leviathan? Political Theology for Modern Times', *Scottish Journal of Theology* 47 (1994): 19–41.

—. *The Crucified God*, trans. R. Wilson and J. Bowdon (London: SCM, 1974).

—. *On Human Dignity: Political Theology and Ethics* (Minneapolis: Augsburg Fortress Press, 1984).

—. *Religion, Revolution and the Future* (New York: Scribner, 1969).

—. *The Spirit of Life: A Universal Affirmation*, trans. M. Kohl (London: SCM, 1992).

—. *Theology of Hope*, trans. J. Leitch (London: SCM, 1967).

Murray, John Courtney. *Bridging the Sacred and the Secular: Selected Writings of John Courtney Murray*, ed. J. Leon Hooper (Washington, DC: Georgetown University Press, 1994).

Myers, Ched. *Binding the Strongman: A Political Reading of Mark's Story of Jesus* (Maryknoll, NY: Orbis, 2008 [1988]).

Neuhaus, Richard John. *The Catholic Moment: The Paradox of the Church in the Postmodern World* (New York: HarperCollins, 1990).

—. *The Naked Public Square: Religion and Democracy in America* (Grand Rapids: Eerdmans, 1984).

Niebuhr, H. Richard. *Christ and Culture* (New York: Harper, 1951).

Niebuhr, Reinhold. *The Essential Reinhold Niebuhr: Selected Essays and Addresses*, ed. Robert McAfee Brown (New Haven, CT: Yale University Press, 1986).

—. *Love and Justice: Selections from the Shorter Writings of Reinhold Niebuhr*, ed. D. B. Robertson (Louisville, KY: Westminster/John Knox Press, 1957).

—. *Moral Man and Immoral Society: A Study of Ethics and Politics* (Louisville, KY: Westminster John Knox Press, 2001).

Novak, David. *Covenantal Rights: A Study in Jewish Political Theory* (Princeton: Princeton University Press, 2000).

Nygren, Anders. *Agape and Eros* (Philadelphia: Westminster, 1953).

Ochs, Peter. 'Abrahamic Theo-politics: A Jewish View', in *The Blackwell Companion to Political Theology* (Oxford: Blackwell, 2004), 519–34.

O'Donovan, Oliver. *The Desire of the Nations: Rediscovering the Roots of Political Theology* (Cambridge: Cambridge University Press, 1996).

—. *The Just War Revisited* (Cambridge: Cambridge University Press, 2003).

—. *The Ways of Judgment* (Grand Rapids: Eerdmans, 2005).

O'Donovan, Oliver and Joan Lockwood O'Donovan. *Bonds of Imperfection: Christian Politics, Past and Present* (Grand Rapids: Eerdmans, 2004).

—, eds. *From Irenaeus to Grotius: A Sourcebook in Christian Political Thought* (Grand Rapids: Eerdmans, 1999).

Oduyoye, Mercy Amba and Musimbi R. A. Kanyoro, eds. *The Will to Arise: Women, Tradition, and the Church in Africa* (Maryknoll, NY: Orbis Press, 1992).

Pecknold, C. C. *Christianity and Politics: A Brief Guide to the History* (Eugene, OR: Cascade Books, 2010).

Phillips, Elizabeth. '"We've Read the End of the Book": An Engagement with Contemporary Christian Zionism through the Eschatology of John Howard Yoder', *Studies in Christian Ethics* 21.3 (2008): 342–61.

Pinnock, Sarah H., ed. *The Theology of Dorothee Soelle* (Harrisburg, PA: Trinity Press International, 2003).

Plekon, Michael. 'Eastern Orthodox Thought', in *The Blackwell Companion to Political Theology* (Oxford: Blackwell, 2004), 93–106.

Porter, Jean. *Natural Law and Divine Law: Reclaiming the Tradition for Christian Ethics* (Grand Rapids: Eerdmans, 1999).

Rahner, Hugo. *Church and State in Early Christianity* (San Francisco: Ignatius Press, 1992).

Rasmussen, Arne. *The Church as Polis: From Political Theology to Theological Politics as Exemplified by Jürgen Moltmann and Stanley Hauerwas* (Notre Dame: University of Notre Dame Press, 1995).

Rawls, John. *A Theory of Justice* (Cambridge, MA: Harvard University Press, 1971).

Roberts, J. Deotis. *A Black Political Theology* (Louisville, KY: Westminster Press, 1974).

Rowland, Christopher. 'Scripture: New Testament', in *The Blackwell Companion to Political Theology* (Oxford: Blackwell, 2004), 21–34.

Ruether, Rosemary Radford. *Christianity and Social Systems: Historical Constructions and Ethical Challenges* (Lanham, MD: Rowman & Littlefield, 2009).

—. *Faith and Fratricide: The Theological Roots of Anti-Semitism* (New York: Seabury Press, 1974).

—. *Gaia and God: An Ecofeminist Theology of Earth Healing* (London: SCM Press, 1992).

—. *Sexism and God-Talk: Toward a Feminist Theology* (Boston, MA: Beacon Press, 1993).

Ruether, Rosemary Radford and Herman J. Ruether. *The Wrath of Jonah: The Crisis of Religious Nationalism in the Israeli-Palestinian Conflict* (Minneapolis: Augsburg Fortress, 2002)

'The Schleitheim Brotherly Union', in *The Legacy of Michael Sattler*, trans. and ed. John Howard Yoder (Scottdale, PA: Herald Press, 1973), 28–54.

Schmitt, Carl. *Political Theology: Four Chapters on the Concept of Sovereignty* (Chicago: University of Chicago Press, 1985).

Schweitzer, Albert. *The Quest of the Historical Jesus*, trans. W. Montgomery (Minneapolis: Fortress, 2001 [1906]).

Scott, Peter and William T. Cavanaugh, eds. *The Blackwell Companion to Political Theology* (Oxford: Blackwell, 2004).

Shirer, William L. *The Rise and Fall of the Third Reich: A History of Nazi Germany* (New York: Touchstone, 1959).

Siemon-Netto, Uwe. 'Goodbye Utopia, Hello Luther! Half a millennium after the Protestant Reformation, American scholars seek advice from its leader', *The Atlantic Times* (December 2006).

Smith, James K. A. *Introducing Radical Orthodoxy: Mapping a Post-secular Theology* (Grand Rapids: Baker Academic, 2004).

Sölle, Dorothee. *Against the Wind: Memoir of a Radical Christian* (Minneapolis: Augsburg Fortress, 1999).

—. *Political Theology* (Philadelphia: Fortress Press, 1974).

Song, Robert. *Christianity and Liberal Society* (Oxford: Oxford University Press, 1997).

Stackhouse, Max. 'Civil Religion, Political Theology and Public Theology: What's the Difference?' *Political Theology* 5.3 (2004): 275–93.

Swift, Louis J. *The Early Fathers on War and Military Service* (Wilmington, DE: Michael Glazier, Inc., 1983).

Taylor, Mark Lewis. 'Spirit', in *The Blackwell Companion to Political Theology* (Oxford: Blackwell, 2004), 377–92.

Theimann, Ronald F. *Constructing a Public Theology: The Church in a Pluralistic Culture* (Louisville: Westminster-John Knox Press, 1991).

—. *Religion in Public Life: A Dilemma for Democracy* (Georgetown: Georgetown University Press/The Century Fund, 1996).

Thompson, J. Milburn. *Introducing Catholic Social Thought* (Maryknoll, NY: Orbis Books, 2010).

Townes, Emilie. *Embracing the Spirit: Womanist Perspectives on Hope, Salvation and Transformation* (Maryknoll, NY: Orbis, 1997).

Tracy, David. *The Analogical Imagination: Christian Theology and the Culture of Pluralism* (New York: Crossroad, 1981).

—. *Blessed Rage for Order: The New Pluralism in Theology* (New York: Seabury, 1975).

Van Nieuwenhove, Rik and Joseph Wawryow, eds. *The Theology of Thomas Aquinas* (Notre Dame: University of Notre Dame Press, 2005).

Ward, Graham. *Christ and Culture* (Oxford: Blackwell, 2005).

—. *Theology and Contemporary Critical Theory*, 2nd edn (London: Macmillan Press Ltd., 2000).

Webster, John, ed. *The Cambridge Companion to Karl Barth* (Cambridge: Cambridge University Press, 2000).

Werpehowski, William. 'Anders Nygren's Agape and Eros', in *The Oxford Handbook of Theological Ethics*, ed. Gilbert Mileander and William Werpehowski (Oxford: Oxford University Press), 433–48.

Williams, Delores S. *Sisters in the Wilderness: The Challenge of Womanist God-Talk* (Maryknoll, NY: Orbis, 1993).

Williams, Rowan. 'Ascension Day', in *Open to Judgement* (London: Darton, Longman & Todd, 1994), 81–5.

—. 'Politics and the Soul: A Reading of the City of God', *Milltown Studies* 19/20 (Spring and Autumn 1987): 55–72.

—, ed. *Sergii Bulgakov: Towards a Russian Political Theology* (Edinburgh: T&T Clark, 1999).

Wink, Walter. *Engaging the Powers: Discernment and Resistance in a World of Domination* (Minneapolis: Fortress Press, 1992).

Yoder, John Howard. 'Armaments and Eschatology', *Studies in Christian Ethics* 1:1 (1988): 43–61.

—. *The Christian Witness to the State* (Faith & Life Press, 1964 and Scottdale, PA: Herald Press, 2002).

—. *For the Nations: Essays Public and Evangelical* (Grand Rapids: Eerdmans, 1997).

—. *The Jewish-Christian Schism Revisited* (London: SCM Press, 2003).

—. *The Politics of Jesus* (Grand Rapids: Eerdmans 1994 [1972]).

—. *Preface to Theology: Christology and Theological Method* (Grand Rapids: Brazos Press, 2002).

—. *The Priestly Kingdom* (Notre Dame: Notre Dame University Press, 1984).

—. *The Royal Priesthood: Essays Ecclesiological and Ecumenical* (Grand Rapids: Eerdmans, 1994).

Zwick, Mark and Louise Zwick. *The Catholic Worker Movement: Intellectual and Spiritual Origins* (Mahwah, NJ: Paulist Press, 2005).

AUTHOR INDEX

SUBJECT INDEX